PORTLANDIA

A GUIDE FOR VISITORS

PORTLANDIA

A GUIDE FOR VISITORS

FRED ARMISEN, CARRIE BROWNSTEIN, JONATHAN KRISEL, BILL OAKLEY, KAREY DORNETTO

GRAND CENTRAL
PUBLISHING

New York • Boston

Grand Central Publishing
Hachette Book Group
237 Park Avenue
New York, NY 10017

www.HachetteBookGroup.com
Printed in the United States of America

Q-MA
First Edition: November 2012
10 9 8 7 6 5 4 3 2 1

Grand Central Publishing is a division of Hachette Book Group, Inc.
The Grand Central Publishing name and logo is a trademark of Hachette Book Group, Inc.

The Hachette Speakers Bureau provides a wide range of authors for speaking events. To find out more, go to www.hachettespeakersbureau.com or call (866) 376-6591.

The publisher is not responsible for websites (or their content) that are not owned by the publisher.

Library of Congress Control Number: 2012940705

ISBN: 978-1-4555-2058-9

This book was printed on 130% recycled paper in a peanut-free, smoke-free plant by local workers in a friendly and fair environment, free of sudden noises and unnatural light. By 130% recycled paper, we mean that any papers touching the paper that this book was printed on were subsequently destroyed and reconstituted for future use in other publications. All ink is made from pure Oregon blueberries. The publishers adhere to a strict "no paper memos" rule throughout the offices, and the front of the building is all bicycle racks. This shouldn't even need to be addressed, but no animal products whatsoever were used in any aspect of the production of this book, even distantly, by vendors, distributors, etc. In fact, prior to publication, portions of this book were read aloud to two horses to see how they reacted. This may seem laughable, but it gave the writers and publishers a sense of calm. The book's spine is made from a cold-pressed mixture of dirt and pine resin. Everything everywhere is fragrance free.

Book design by HRoberts Design

Last-Minute Changes

Please note that in Portlandia street names can change overnight, or block by block. We apologize for any confusion. For up to the minute, need-to-know information, please never need to get anywhere.

As of this printing, NE 20th has been renamed Howard Zinn Boulevard (except for the parts of SE 20th between Division and Hawthorne, where the change is still being disputed on account of whether everyone who lives on the street actually needs to have read *A People's History of the United States*).

On the last Tuesday of every month, streets that begin with the letter *M* are required to have a drum circle that lasts no less than four hours.

NE Prescott Street has been renamed Kurt Cobain Lane. [*Editor's note:* This guidebook does not recognize this name change, since Kurt Cobain is from Washington State, and is only noting it for the sake of veracity.] When you get to Portlandia, please pick up a petition, started by us, to change "Prescott" to "Nu Shooz" instead.

The area between SE Belmont and SE Stark has seceded from Portlandia and will now be known as The Real Portlandia, not to be confused with the area between NE Alberta and NE Ainsworth, which has also registered the name The Real Portlandia.

SW 5th through SW 9th Avenues are currently being renamed by cats. The city awaits the services of animal communicator Susanna Vapnek, who will translate the felines' wishes into monikers that we humans can understand. As of now, the street signs are blank, save for a small paw print.

E. Burnside between 7th and 10th Streets no longer has a name and is now just a feeling.

CONTENTS

Welcome to Portlandia

Portlandia is the dream of the '90s—in a very literal sense. In 1991 a government bond initiative was put on the ballot to revitalize the city. State senator Dave Jorn had a dream that the city would transform from a run-down manufacturing town and become a shining jewel in the beautiful emerald forest. It passed. And that dream, signed into law in 1993, became reality in 2012.

We are proud to show off all of our new bells and whistles:

See Big Pink, the largest and only high-rise in Portlandia. Come for the thousands of square feet of unused office space, stay for the revolving restaurant on the 16th floor. Come see Women and Women First, the largest feminist bookstore in the world. Come see Lipsey Park, the public park where each landscaping choice has a plaque explaining its allusion to a historic event in Portlandia's past. Come see the many rivers and bodies of water on which to enjoy all manner of inflatable sporting apparatuses.

Hi, I'm Fred.
I'm Carrie.
WELCOME!

Wait, wait, wait…is this going to be confusing? What? Which one of us is talking? I don't think it matters. No, it totally matters. Everything matters, Carrie. You're right, Fred. It matters as much as the beautiful cloud formations in a crisp summer Portlandia sky. It matters like the right of a fly to live in that Portlandia sky without fear of being swatted down. Yes! Everything in Portlandia matters. So…I'll go first. Why, "ladies first"? Don't be insensitive, buddy. Don't call me "buddy," buddy. Sorry, that wasn't cool. We're not being cool. Fred, you go first. Okay, thanks.

Hi, I'm Fred. WELCOME! Wait—I can't. It doesn't feel right. I feel bad about the whole "ladies first" thing. I mean, as a feminist, a pacifist, an animal lover, an outdoorsman, an indoorsman, an ex-door-to-door-salesman-against-door-to-door-salesmen, and an ironic vegan foodie, I—I just can't. This is a terrible way to start the book. It's like, what kind of message are we going to give people? That we fight in Portlandia. That's not true. No, this is a place where everyone is welcome. Even if you shot a bear in cold blood or accidentally killed him by feeding him honey only to find out he's allergic…Portlandia would be like, "Come on in, dude! We welcome you!" Wait…I wouldn't go that far, Fred. We love bears, insects, even pickled pickles. Carrie, I've been meaning to tell you something. Remember that camping trip I took in Forest Park? Yeah… Well, I was too scared that I would be attacked by a grizzly or a tourist from Seattle…so I ended up not going. Thanks for being honest, Fred. It's okay to be a baby in Portlandia, even if you're a man. In fact, we love it! And if you're a woman…you're allowed to be old! Grow that long gray hair out! Now we're having fun—right, Fred? Yes, Carrie!

Look, we want you to have fun. Be yourself, whatever that may be. We only have one rule: Be nice, eat rice and don't think twice!

Fred, did you just make that up? It doesn't make sense. I didn't say it. You did. Oh, right. It doesn't make sense. But who cares.

WE DON'T!!!

So get on in there. Turn the page. Slow or fast or not at all—we're cool with whatever. We love you! Well…mostly we love Portlandia. And that's the important thing.

XOXO (and ABCDEFGHIJKLMNPQRSTUVWYZ— we wouldn't want to leave you guys out, either), —Fred and Carrie

Beauty…
Passion…
A shining pearl in the clam of the Northwest.

Flowers…
Bridges…
'Tis the fairest city in all thee land.

Me beloved brethren of the realm
Come take a cool drink at thy city

This is Portlandia!!!

—The Mayor

From the Industrial-Looking
Brushed Stainless-Steel Worktable of
THE MAYOR

Good afternoon! I hope this book finds you sitting comfortably in a love seat or on a sectional couch with your feet propped up. Of all of my tasks as Governing Mayor, overseeing production of this official Guidebook for Visitors has been at the top of my list of priorities. Our head of tourism, Adriana Mustain, presented me with some examples of travel guides from various cities around the country. I found most of them to be uninspired and perfunctory. Here's an important statue, this is a good shopping area, blah, blah, blah. Seattle's was the most disposable. Ordinary maps with endless arrows and stars, pointing out the most obvious landmarks. Come and see the Space Needle? Really? I had no idea! As a side note, I would like to point out that our city has a Space Needle as well. We just refuse to advertise it. It's called the Hi-Point, and it's about the same height as the Seattle attraction. Maybe a little shorter. It is a truly beautiful structure. But you won't find it on any of our maps or anywhere in this book. We don't do that here. We even ask visitors not to talk about the Hi-Point once they return to their city of origin! In my opinion, it has been a very successful anti-campaign.

There are some wonderful entries in these pages from some of our favorite local artists; I hope you enjoy them. We tried to include as many aspects of this city as we could, but I'm sure we didn't get it all. My hope is that future editions of this guidebook will correct those omissions.

If you decide to visit, please feel welcome. You will be treated not as a tourist but as a temporary citizen. We Portlandians are not overly friendly, and you will thank us for that. I think that being friendly, and especially *claiming* to be friendly, is an overrated trait when it comes to travel destinations. We will greet you with a smile, point you in the direction of whatever you are looking for, and then leave you alone to enjoy the city on your own terms.

We included some maps in this book, but you can ignore them if you make your way here. This is a great place to get lost in. Just put on a light jacket, bring some music, and start walking. Anywhere. You'll love it, I promise.

If you're looking for me, I'm around. Feel free to stop by and say hi. Seriously. I'm either at City Hall or riding around on my bike. From the bottom of my heart, welcome to Portlandia!

**Love,
The Mayor**

[*Editor's note*: Because this book respects all voices, we have included this rebuttal letter to The Mayor's welcome.]

Dear Reader:

Thank you for your interest in our fair city. And what a nice Mayor we have who would extend such a gracious welcome. By no means am I here to discourage you from visiting. That's not what this letter is about. At *all*. However, I just wanted to say that you might also want to consider NOT visiting.

For as many reasons as there are to take a trip to Portlandia, there might be more reasons for you to *never*, ever do that. Here's an obvious one: the environmental impact. Something to ask yourself: "What size shoe does my carbon footprint wear?" (That's actually a trick question, because most of us in Portlandia go barefoot, especially while standing in line at the bank or dancing to Brazilian psych music at house parties.) Flying or driving into a city as eco-conscious as ours— and using vast amounts of fuel and polluting the air while doing so—is utterly irresponsible. In fact, it contradicts one of the very reasons you're likely visiting, which is to convince yourself that you enjoy nature. It's true, nature is a wonderful place to meditate about the beer you'll drink when the hike is over, or to think about the most poetic Twitter update you can write once your cell phone comes back into range. And just so you know, by the time you read this, it might be illegal to get to Portlandia by any means other than crawling, canoe, or bicycle. (For more info on this, check out my blog.)

Another reason not to visit is that by doing so you will irrevocably change this city. Do you want to be responsible for that? Have you discussed what that burden will feel like with your therapist, Reiki practitioner, or astrologer? Have you heard of the Observer's Paradox? Basically, it means that by coming here to study and learn about Portlandians, you can't help but change us. Want to observe us in our natural environment? Then stay home and read about us reading *The New York Times* in *The New York Times*.

Also, I have to ask: Are you bringing contraband or invasive species into this city? Contraband includes but is not limited to: wheat, hair dye, California, a PhD, confident driving skills, and any album other than the first album. Invasive species include: purebred dogs and, most likely, you.

Lastly, please ask yourself this: do you belong here and/or deserve to be in Portlandia? If you answered yes, then you don't.

See you online.

**Respectfully,
Kenneth Richards
(Portlandia native
of 3 years)**

Things You Should Read Before Coming to Portlandia

Or, How to Be an Educated Portlandian and Not Look Bad at a Party

- This book!!! Hello??
- The most recent *New Yorker*—from front to back, not just the cartoons and movie reviews
- *What's the Matter with Kansas? How the Conservatives Won the Heart of America*, by Thomas Frank
- *Veganomicon: The Ultimate Vegan Cookbook*
- *Mayoral Musings*, by The Mayor of Portlandia
- *Live From New York: An Uncensored History of Saturday Night Live*—we like sketch comedy in Portlandia
- *The Handbook of Good English*—we also like you to speak well
- Everything by David Sedaris, Sarah Vowell, and Dave Eggers
- *Between a Rock and a Hard Place*, by Aron Ralston—the climber who cut his arm off. Portlandia is surrounded by woods. If you need to escape or we're chasing you out (which we probably wouldn't, unless you were really mean), you'll need to have some survival knowledge…and inspirational reading.
- *Conversations with Woody Allen*
- The complete works of Shakespeare

This should keep you pretty busy.

Key to Symbols Used in This Guidebook

LODGING

Backpacker accessible

Multilingual staff

Classic bellhops

Cool bellboys

Rustic accommodations

Faux rustic accommodations

Ice machine

Ironic ice machine

SHOPPING

Good for gifts

Good for gifts (last-minute)

Good for gifts (returns

Clothing for women

Clothing for womyn

Clothing for grrls

PARK

Frisbee friendly **Ultimate Frisbee friendly** **Frisbee golf friendly**

Picnic friendly **Nudity friendly** **Friend friendly** **Contains restroom** **Restroom (not totally disgusting)**

Band shell **Public art** **Public art (w/o bird excrement)**

25% Homeless/Non homeless ratio **50% Homeless**

75% Homeless **100% Homeless (aka campsite)**

Watch for dog poop **Watch for goose poop**

Water feature **Water feature (toxic)** **Romantic** **Good for cruising**

DINING OUT

Vegetarian

Vegan

Freegan

Sea-gan

Full bar

Biker bar
(gas-powered)

Biker bar
(human powered)

Biker bar
(fixies only)

Wheelchair accessibly

Skateboard accessible

Segway accessible

Casual attire

Clothing optional

Polyamorous

LGBTQ

Pet friendly

Dog friendly

Cat friendly

Mouse friendly

For dogs (only)

Child friendly

Child tolerant

Child indifferent

Child hostile

Regionally sourced food

Regionally sourced waitstaff

Locally sourced food

House-sourced

Accepts credit cards

Accepts cash

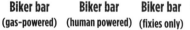
Accepts barter

Accepts positive vibes

PARK

Frisbee friendly **Ultimate Frisbee friendly** **Frisbee golf friendly**

Picnic friendly **Nudity friendly** **Friend friendly** **Contains restroom** **Restroom (not totally disgusting)**

Band shell **Public art** **Public art (w/o bird excrement)**

25% Homeless/Non homeless ratio **50% Homeless**

75% Homeless **100% Homeless (aka campsite)**

Watch for dog poop **Watch for goose poop**

Water feature **Water feature (toxic)** **Romantic** **Good for cruising**

DINING OUT

 Vegetarian

 Vegan

 Freegan

 Sea-gan

 Full bar

 Biker bar (gas-powered)

 Biker bar (human powered)

 Biker bar (fixies only)

 Wheelchair accessibly

Skateboard accessible

 Segway accessible

 Casual attire

 Clothing optional

 Polyamorous

LGBTQ

 Pet friendly

 Dog friendly

 Cat friendly

 Mouse friendly

 For dogs (only)

 Child friendly

 Child tolerant

 Child indifferent

Child hostile

 Regionally sourced food

 Regionally sourced waitstaff

 Locally sourced food

 House-sourced

 Accepts credit cards

 Accepts cash

 Accepts barter

 Accepts positive vibes

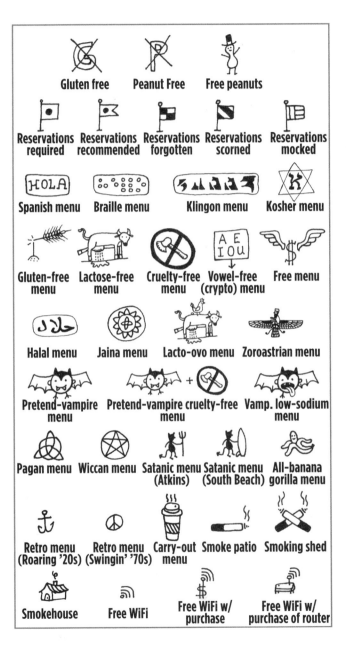

Gluten free Peanut Free Free peanuts

Reservations required Reservations recommended Reservations forgotten Reservations scorned Reservations mocked

Spanish menu Braille menu Klingon menu Kosher menu

Gluten-free menu Lactose-free menu Cruelty-free menu Vowel-free (crypto) menu Free menu

Halal menu Jaina menu Lacto-ovo menu Zoroastrian menu

Pretend-vampire menu Pretend-vampire cruelty-free menu Vamp. low-sodium menu

Pagan menu Wiccan menu Satanic menu (Atkins) Satanic menu (South Beach) All-banana gorilla menu

Retro menu (Roaring '20s) Retro menu (Swingin' '70s) Carry-out menu Smoke patio Smoking shed

Smokehouse Free WiFi Free WiFi w/ purchase Free WiFi w/ purchase of router

Chapter One

Northeast Portlandia

Chapter One

· ·

Northeast Portlandia

Introduction

By Doug and Claire

Ugh, when was the last time we even went out? We used to do a lot of stuff in NE. Doug, what's that one bar? With the whiskey flights and the in-house jug band? They had that great guy who played rhythm triangle and everyone thought he should play lead? There's also that cool barbershop that used to be "walk-ins only" and then they switched to "walk-in reservations only," and then for a while you were only allowed to "walk by." They closed for a month to install wood flooring repurposed from an old basketball court, which replaced flooring salvaged from an old elementary school, then they reopened with the same owner, different gender.

Anyhow, we're sort of the wrong people to ask about our neighborhood. Last year we got obsessed with *Battlestar Galactica* and watched the entire series in a matter of weeks. Or was it days? It's all a blur. And the antibiotics I was on—for the inevitable bladder infection caused by not getting up from the couch for days on end—left me a little hazy on the details. I CAN tell you all of the places that offer delivery service in NE. (Wait, almost no one delivers in all of Portlandia, except for the US Postal Service, a handful of pizza chains, a memory-foam mattress outlet via bike, and the library.) Our neighbor Tom has been really great about bringing over supplies while we get through this

phase in our lives. And it is just a phase. There aren't that many TV shows to watch, right?

You'll love NE Portlandia!

Best,
Doug and Claire

NE

NE

An Interview with the Owner of The Knot Store

Q = Interviewer

KSO = Knot Store Owner

Q: Hi.

KSO: Hello.

Q: Is it okay that I put my recorder on top of your glass counter?

KSO: Of course. What is that, a digital recorder?

Q: Yes.

KSO: *Picking it up.* Ahhhhhhhh.

Q: Yeah.

KSO: They just get smaller and smaller, don't they.

Q: This one is already a few years old.

KSO: Olympus. I'm going to write down the name.

Q: Okay.

KSO: *Looking for a pen.* Let me find a pen.

Q: Sure.

KSO: Ah, I have one in the back. Wait here a second. One second. *He leaves.*

Q: *Looks around and sees many knots. Little segments of rope, all the same size. Some framed,*

NE

Artesan Knots

COMPLETE PRICE LIST

Running Bowline **$35**

Lark's Head **$55**

Lariat Loop **$42**

Double Hitch **$55**

Double Overhand Noose **$75**

Figure Eight **$80**

Overhand Bend **$35**

Bumper **$79**

Double Fisherman **$99**

Overhand **$35**

Cowboy Bowline **$95**

Granny Knot **$85**

Lark's Head Reverse **$45**

Fisherman's Knot **$120**

Sailor's Hitch **$75**

Trident Loop **$55**

Portuguese Bowline **$55**

some on display out in the open. Names like Lark's Head, Butterfly Coil.

A little bell above the front door jingles and a normal-looking woman with red hair appears.

NLWWRH: Hi! Is he in?

Q: He's in the back.

NLWWRH: Oh, he's busy. Tell him that I'll just meet him at lunch.

Q: Okay. *She leaves.*

KSO: *Walking back in.* Got one. Olympus. *Writes it on a notepad.*

Q: A woman was just here and she said she'd meet you at lunch?

KSO: Amanda! Oh, good!

Q: So should I just start?

KSO: Whenever you're ready.

Q: What gave you the idea to start a knot store?

KSO: What gave me the idea?

Q: Yes.

KSO: I had been interested in knots right out of high school and began collecting them. I discovered that there was a very well-connected network of knot aficionados around the world, and pretty soon, I found myself communicating with them. Trading knots. Learning about new knots. Naming them. Even arguing about the validity of some knots.

Q: That's an issue?

KSO: Of course it is! You can't just tie two ends of rope together and call it a knot. There are *rules*.

Q: Like what?

KSO: Ahhhhhhh. That is something that takes a lifetime of education to know. Knots go all the way back to before there were books!

The bell above the front door jingles and the normal-looking woman with red hair pokes her head in.

Amanda: *She smiles and shows the Knot Store Owner a large white cardboard envelope.*

KSO: You got it! I can't wait to see it. I bet it's great.

A: I'll see you at lunch.

KSO: I'll see you at lunch.

She leaves.

Q: Where did you grow up?

KSO: A little bit outside of here. But here.

Q: Did you do any other jobs before you had this store?

KSO: Nope.

Q: This is all you've ever done?

KSO: Yup.

Q: You never worked anyplace? Or ran another kind of business?

NE

KSO: Nope.

Q: Are you interested in anything else?

KSO: Of course.

Q: Like?

KSO: Hammer Films—you know, from England. Just beautiful, moody films. Very interesting. New York salsa music. From the '70s. It's called Boogaloo, do you know it?

Q: No.

KSO: Amazing piano work. I can't get enough of it. Here, let me play you some. *He turns around and presses play on a small sound system. Raw salsa music is heard.* This is Ocho. Listen to that.

Q: That's incredible.

KSO: *Turns down music.*

Q: But knots are your passion.

KSO: I would say that, yes. And I'm still learning about knots. The history is overwhelming. From country to country, too. I love it. I don't even think of this store as a workplace!

Q: That's amazing.

KSO: Let me show you around. Look at this one. Right here. The loop is somehow a square... *He proceeds to show the interviewer around the knot store, describing each knot in detail.*

NE

Adult Babysitting Services

ELLEN 503·555·0274

Adult Babysitting Services

Does your husband, wife, partner, boyfriend, girlfriend, or the person you are currently sharing a bed with behave like a child? Do you have a job and they don't? Do you need to make sure when you get home from a hard day they're not drunk or in a video-game coma? If you answered yes to any of the above, then ABS can help you.

All of our sitters have been in failed long-term relationships involving someone like your adult in need. They understand how to handle: laziness, whiny backtalk, overbearing mothers, excuses for why they didn't go and look for a job today, obsessive Internet use, obsessive Internet porn use, and unhealthy eating habits, such as Skittles and Dr. Brown's root beer for breakfast.

For only $10 an hour, one of our qualified adult sitters will take care of all your big baby's needs. For an extra $10, our sitters will tutor and monitor daily exercise. All sitters are proficient in Wii, Xbox, PlayStation, TiVo and DVR systems, everything Apple, and Gawker Media.

Hi Ellen.

THANKS FOR STAYING HERE AND TAKING CARE OF DOUG. PLEASE MAKE YOURSELF AT HOME.

-DOUG NEEDS TO HAVE SOMETHING OTHER THAN SODA WITH HIS DINNER. HE'S MORE LIKELY TO DRINK WATER OUT OF HIS FAVORITE GLASS, WHICH IS THE ONE WITH THE "SHORT CIRCUIT" MOVIE LOGO ON IT.

-DOUG IS ALLOWED TWO BEERS, OR ONE BEER AND ONE SWEET. DON'T LET HIM CONVINCE YOU THAT GREEN TEA ICE-CREAM OR CHOCOLATE COUNT AS ANTI-OXIDANTS AND NOT AS DESSERT. HE CAN BE VERY PERSUASIVE, ESPECIALLY AFTER A BEER. ALSO, HE WILL TRY FOR THREE BEERS BUT PLEASE BE FIRM.

-DON'T LET HIM FILL UP ON SNACKS, EVEN THE ONES CLAIMING TO CONTAIN FLAX OR ACAI.

-NO MORE THAN ONE HOUR OF VIDEO GAMES. REMIND HIM THAT THE SUB-WOOFER IS NOT NEEDED FOR WINNING.

-NO FACEBOOK UPDATES OR TWEETS THAT MENTION MY HYPOCHONDRIA OR THAT USE THE WORDS "ANY RECOS?"

-DRUMS ARE FINE BUT NOT AFTER 10 PM. AND DON'T LET HIM ENGAGE YOU IN A GAME OF "NAME THAT DRUM FILL." THIS INEVITABLY LEADS TO LECTURES ABOUT THE CLASH. BOW WOW WOW AND THE GRATUITOUS USE OF THE WORDS "PARADIDDLE" AND "FLAM."

-PLEASE DON'T LET HIM WRITE REVIEWS ON MUSIC BLOGS OR MAKE COMMENTS ON ON-LINE MOVIE DATABASES FOR FILMS THAT ARE STILL IN PRODUCTION.

-DOUG CANNOT GO TO BED WEARING A COAT OR ANY OTHER OUTERWEAR.

-IF HE'S BEEN GOOD, PLEASE READ HIM SOMETHING FROM BOING BOING. OR LET HIM BROWSE THE NEW APPS FOR HIS iPAD. THOSE THINGS HELP HIM RELAX AND FALL ASLEEP.

-I'D LIKE HIM TO GO DOWN AROUND 11 PM.

DON'T HESITATE TO CALL ME ON MY CELL PHONE IF YOU HAVE ANY QUESTIONS OR CONCERNS.

THANKS AGAIN,
CLAIRE

NE

*Welson
Lightbulbs*

*Come in and look around. But please don't
slam the door behind you when you leave.*   *NW Wilson and 24th*

Wilson Lightbulbs

We specialize in handmade bulbs. Electricity can be taken for granted in this day and age. We admire mixed drinks based on old recipes, we admire haircuts—or the lack thereof—based on styles from the turn of the 20th century. Why not complete your picture of that bygone time with a flickering bulb that lasts for only a few hours and is completely unstable? I blow the glass on each bulb personally. Warning: The waitlist is extremely long. Sorry! I got into the bulbmaking business for the love of the craft and I'm hoping your interest is a passing fancy, since I can't really be trusted to complete anything in a timely manner. I am actually as surprised as the rest of you out there that this is enabling me to earn a living. However, I am using the waitlist and my apparent busy-ness to take as many breaks as possible. Coffee breaks, tea breaks, walks around the block. My assistant, Darby, can take your name and number, required wattage, and bulb color on any day that she doesn't call in sick.

FUN FACT: Each year, Portlandia has 4 Nude Bike Rides, 6 Nude Renaissance Fairs, 2 Nude Oktoberfests, 1 Nude Rodeo, and 46 Nude Bar Mitzvahs.

Listings

Shopping

NE

 ## SONAR HAIR AND RECORDS

1224 NE Killingsworth

Tucked away inside a refurbished nuclear submarine in the heart of NE Portlandia is Sonar Hair and Records. Blind master barber Ponch D'Amico will cut your hair while you browse and shop our store of wacky vintage WWII memorabilia...and records.

 ## JUST SAYING JOKE SHOP

5331 NE Sandy Boulevard

Knock, knock. Who's there? Anybody. Anybody who? Anybody who says anything racist, sexist, ageist, classist, looksist, Eurocentrist, phallist, or ist-ist is not funny. In this store the joke will never be on you... unless you're from Seattle. *Disclaimer: Nothing is funny in this store.*

DID YOU KNOW: A freewheeling city on a majestic river, Portlandia is just like New Orleans but with all the Cajun, African, Caribbean, French, Spanish, and Creole influences replaced by those of young, semi-neurotic white people.

HOME FARMING BOUTIQUE

1439 NE Alberta

Need donkey diapers? Hee-haw! You've come to the right place. Chicken igloos? Bok bok! They've got 'em. Cow collars? Moo! Come on down. Potbelly pig citronella spray to stop those piggies from oinking? You better oinking believe it! Stock up here on designer products to pamper those little farm princes and princesses that are destroying your backyard and your neighbors' lives.

Food & Drink

BROOKLYN EXPAT BARS

Various Locations

Tired of telling your war stories about living in Brooklyn, New York, to impress your friends? Great! Come to one of the many Brooklyn expat bars around town and maintain the edge you received while living in Brooklyn for two weeks. Find the L train crowd on Morrison, the G train on Martin Luther King Boulevard, and the J train on Columbia.

NE

NE

Mixology Menu

The Classic
The Olde Classic
The Gentleman's Fancy
The Plain Speakeasy
The Fancy Plain Specialman
The Judge's Secret Verdict
Mrs. Kentucky Derby
The 51 And Over Club
The Alerted Tycoon
A "Water" On The Rocks

Bachelor's Pantry

1468 NE Prescott

Remember those days when you had no money and could barely afford a free packet of mustard? This is a gourmet twist on those salad days. Nab a pack of nabs or a popcorn cake with red pepper jam (a fun play on the traditional PB&J). Fill up on pinto bean–and–baking soda rice pilaf or olive juice–and–crouton soup. Chef Jimmy Kim will take whatever's in the way way way *way* back of your pantry and fridge, smack it up, flip it over, and rub it down into something nearly ed-ible. You have to come in and see it to believe it. No parties greater than one al-lowed.

For Adults Only

NE

 # STEVE DWYER'S HOUSE

1631 SE 25th Avenue, 2nd floor, NE corner

Steve invites all liberal-minded ladies to join him for a drink or a bowl and see what develops. No pressure, but hey, you only live once, right? Open your mind and maybe your body to the many wonders of Steve. Hours: 6 p.m. to 3 a.m. daily, except when Steve has kickboxing class or his old lady is in town. No cover.

 # STRIP & SOAK

205 NE Multnomah

Leer away those washday blues at Portlandia's first full-service gentlemen's club and laundromat, featuring 32 washers, 48 dryers, and 8 to 12 lusty ladies, depending on time of day. Dry cleaning available. No bedspreads or carpets, please.

FUN FACT: Portlandia is North America's largest consumer of edible mulch.

NE

THE BRUNCH MENU

Salmon benedict with triple orange infused hollandaise and challah bread $15

3 Bacon omelette with side of rosemary potato pancakes, topped with a poached egg $12

Blackened catfish scramble with Cuban rice and yuca butter. $18

House made granola with house made yogurt $4.20

Our famous Marionberry pancakes with pure syrup
2 stack, 5 stack, 6 stack, 8 stack $8-25

For kids only!
Mini bento box Japanese breakfast with small green tea! $8
Lil' salmon scramble! $8
House made granola with house made yogurt $4.20

Orange juice, Banana juice, Peanut milk, coffee, green tea, black tea, pine needle tea $2

EAT-OR-DIE

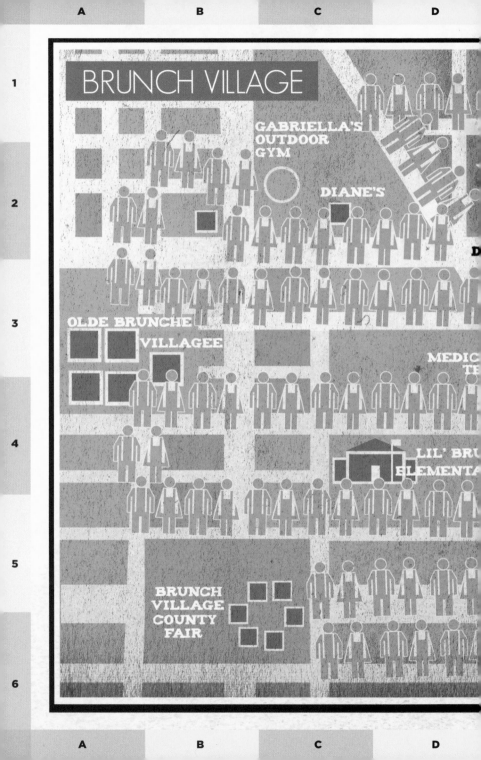

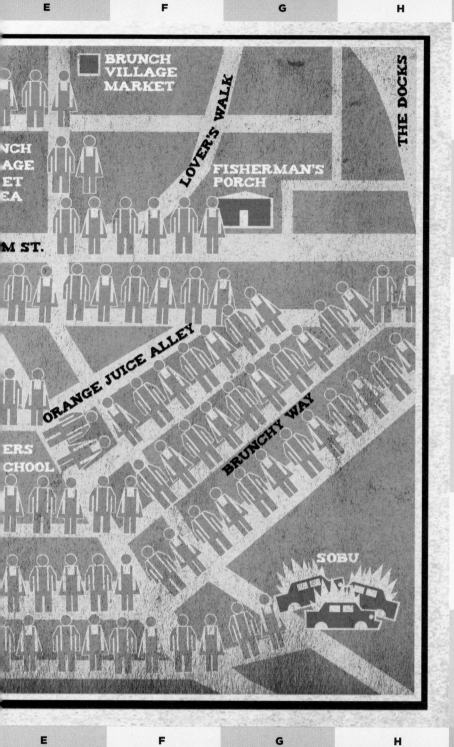

Bring Your Dog to Portlandia!

No question about it: Portlandia is Dog City USA! Though Detroit is #1 for roaming packs of wild dogs, and Shreveport is #1 for dog-processing and canning facilities, Portlandia is America's #1 city for live-pet dog ownership![*]

And the pampered pooches live the good life. From city-subsidized organic dog food to state-subsidized dog parks to county-subsidized dog yoga instruction, the city boasts a wide range of dining and entertainment options for dogs. That's because, in a very real way, dogs are substitute children to Portlandians—many of whom are infertile or impotent or simply unwilling to commit to a mature adult relationship.[**]

Just as you might see a French poodle on its owner's lap in a trendy Champs-Élysées café, you might see a Portlandian hound sitting with its human companion at the movies or taking a discreet whiz in the corner of a quiet coffee shop.

Cat lovers might say the city has gone to the dogs! A less pathetic group might come up with something less clichéd. We may never know.

---

[*]Based on poll of casual acquaintances, 2012

[**] Based on poll of casual acquaintances, 2012

Q: Where Can I Take My Dog?

- NW Surgery Clinic *(Dogs welcome during bi-opsy phase and MRI. Must wear scrubs during surgery.)*
- Federal court
- County court *(All misdemeanor, traffic, divorce, and small claims courts welcome well-behaved dogs. Felony cases at judge's discretion, but most judges LOVE dogs.)*
- County jail and state prison *(Small dogs ONLY during solitary confinement)*
- Abandoned house at 15302 SE 122nd Avenue
- BarkSpace Theater Lab for Dogs
- Temple Beth Emanu-El
- Portlandia State University *(Per health code, dogs only allowed in cafeteria during operating hours)*
- The Wedding Suite at Nordstrom
- City Dog Baths and Steam Room
- All nightclubs, bars, and music venues *(Dogs must be 21 years of age in dog years)*
- UrbanDoggz Dog Tanning Salon
- Budget Dog & Kid DayCare Warehouse *(License currently under review)*
- Portlandia Museum of Fine Art & Dog Wash
- Intel Microchip Design Clean Rom

Dogs Absolutely Not Allowed:

- Fido McWoof's K-9 FunTown & Dogstravaganza

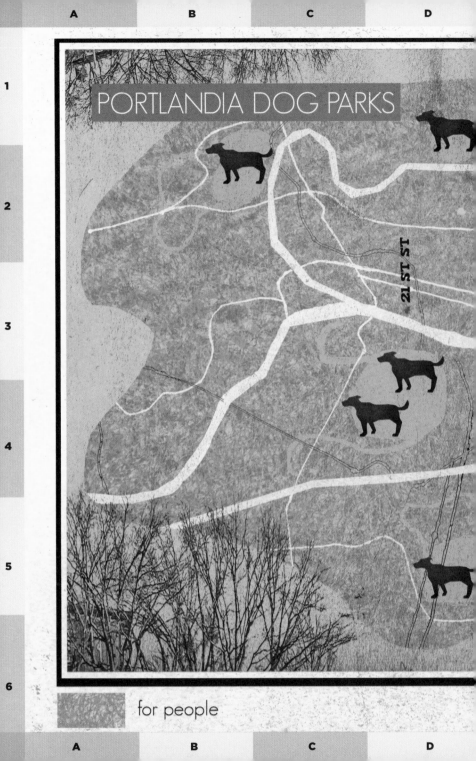

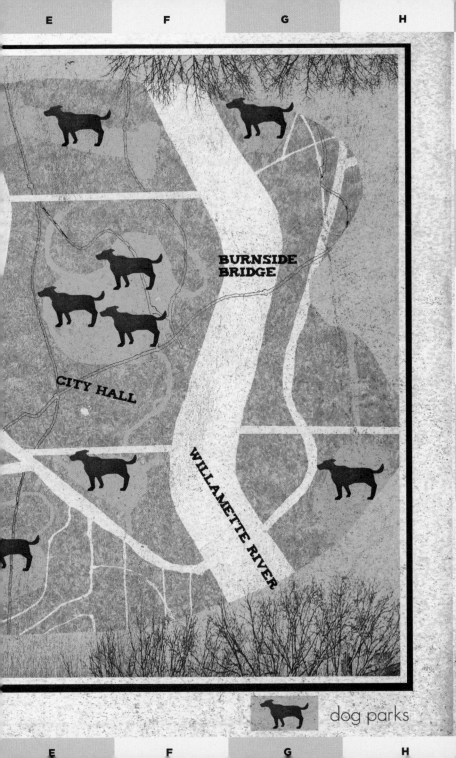

dog parks

PORTLANDIA DOG PARKS
PROJECTED 2016

21 ST ST

for people

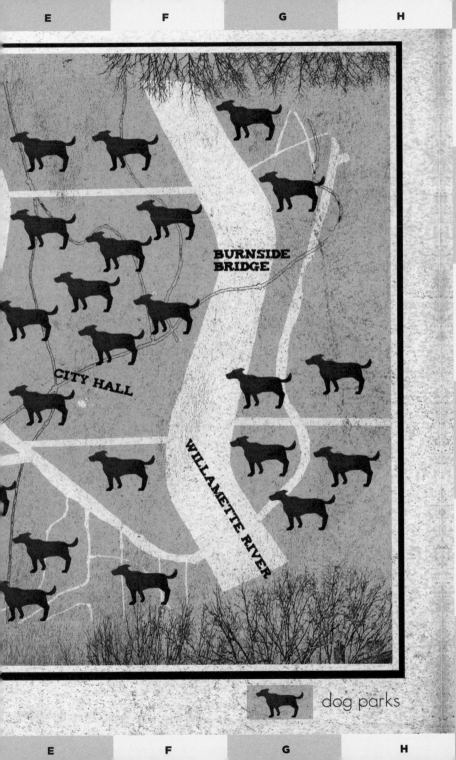

BURNSIDE
BRIDGE

CITY HALL

WILLAMETTE RIVER

dog parks

doG/Park!

NW 8th & Northrup

In 2009, a team of dog-owning ad execs, on-line creatives, and bald guys with goatees and chunky eyeglasses decided to radically redefine our stagnant definition of what a dog park could be. The result was doG/Park!, a "dedicated urban petspace" that "renegotiates the context of outdoor play." The $14 million, quarter-acre park won numerous urban-planning awards and caused a budget shortfall, which resulted in layoffs of 35% of the city's teachers and 911 operators.

Multnomah Romping Grounds

NW 21st Avenue & Glisan

The city's oldest and most exclusive dog park, MRG was founded in 1898 by dental-floss baron Asa P. Oraglide and christened with a stream of glistening gold urine by his bulldog Mick Nipper. Features include a 24-hour squirrel concierge and stick-storage lockers. Membership is restricted to purebreds, though rescue dogs may be considered with two references and evidence of extraordinary heroics. There is currently a 25-year waiting list, so insiders advise applying shortly after your puppy's conception and freezing the fertilized embryo until further notice.

Cascadia Waterfront Skate or Dog Park & Fishing Area (plus R/C Airstrip)

SE 1st Avenue & Salmon

The city's new Cascadia Park enjoys a one-of-a-kind scenic location on the banks of the Willamette. When it opened, skateboarders and dog owners, as well as fishermen and remote-control aircraft enthusiasts, claimed it as their own—and in a Portlandian spirit of conciliation, The Mayor proclaimed that it "belonged equally to all." Subsequent frequent fistfights, concussions, bites, crashes, accidental blindings, and fishhook impalements caused The Mayor to reconsider, though he decided he was happy with his original decision.

Ross Island Mud Pit

South of Ross Island Bridge, off McLoughlin Boulevard

The ultimate in frisky-time fun: a huge, shallow pit filled with muddy runoff from a nearby gravel operation. Infested with rats and has an unbearable stench. Voted "Best Dog Park" 1997–2011.*

*In online poll of computer-using dogs

Portlandia for Dogs

By "Bukowski"

Woof woof pant pant pant pant pant pant pant pant woof woof arf. Arf pant pant pant lick lick lick scratch pant sniff.

Sniff sniff sniff pant pant arr arr WOOF WOOF WOOF! ARF! ARF! Bow wow bow wow!

DID YOU KNOW: Dog baptisms are up 4 percent since 2010 in Portlandia, while cat circumcisions are down 32 percent.

Grr grr grr pant pant pant pant pant pant pant. Pant. Pant. Pant pant pant lick lick lick scratch. Sniff? Sniff?

Pant pant sniff sniff grr sniff scratch and, of course, no visit to the city is complete without a trip to **Pok Pok** (3226 SE Division). Arf!

About the Author

Bukowski is a sheltie-lab mix who can often be found poking his nose into a gopher hole at the NE Portlandia Dog Park. He works in social media marketing and branding.

Chapter Two

Northwest Portlandia

NW

Introduction

**By Nina
(Lance refused
to participate,
but he's still my
honey bunny)**

The best part about living in Northwest Portlandia is that my bad boy beau, Lance, is here with me. Right, Lance? He's out back smoking a cigarette and tinkering on his truck so he can't—Oh, he said he's not "tinkering," he's *modifying his vehicle*. Oooh, that sounds macho. Make a girl blush!

There may be lots to do in NW Portlandia, but Lance and I would rather stay in bed all day making love. Did someone say "cacao"? Not me. *Cacao* is still our safe word but Lance knows just what I like now, so we never have to use it. He's so soft and sweet. Sigh. Nina, *that's me*, is one lucky redheaded girl. After we make love, we like to stay in bed for hours, staring into each other's eyes. Lance has the dreamiest brownies. That's what I call his eyes—isn't that cute? I know.

When Lance pops the question (check our Facebook page for details)—HINT, HINT—I suspect it will be at our local Trader Joe's. We originally met in the nut aisle. I was wistfully looking at the sesame-crusted cashews—I became allergic in my twenties—when Lance walked up and said, "Move, lady." He bumped right into me. I yelped "Ouch," and he said "Ugh," and we've been together ever since. And you thought James Cameron's *Titanic* was romantic. Move over Rose and Jack, there's a new couple in town. I'm kidding. No, I'm not. I think Lance is done smoking—I'm going to

NW

go sneak some pics of him all sweaty. But these are 4myEYESonly. Wink, wink.

**Clear eyes, full
heart (for Lance),
can't lose,
Nina**

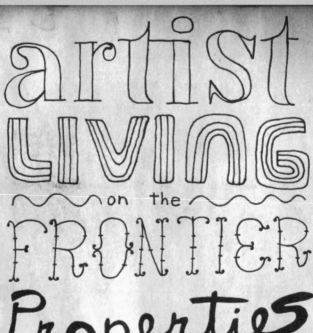

artist
LIVING
on the
FRONTIER
Properties

NW

**Y**ou are looking for a place to live. You are looking to go a little bit out of your way to get something more affordable. You want something that says, "I am not ostentatious." A place that says, "I found the coolest little gem, I was the lucky one." It has supercheap rent and tons of character. It's probably owned by an Eastern European immigrant who doesn't seem to understand the value of the property. Inside it's cozy and cute with brightly colored walls, on the outside it's crumbling, with visible signs of tough teenage vandalism. The place is a clear representation to all of your friends and acquaintances that you got into the neighborhood before the waves of gentrification swept through and homogenized everything, everything that made the place cool and edgy in the first place.

Welcome to Artist Living on the Frontier Properties! We specialize in brand-new properties that maintain the dilapidated look of lower-income areas that were the initial draw for "poor" college students, artists, people not looking to work, and musicians. Yes, you want the danger, the bohemian reclamation of space, the struggle—but without the struggle. Who needs the hassle of dealing with bad plumbing or the inconvenience of outdated outlets without the third prong? You may be a professional, actually making money, but it shouldn't look like you are. No one wants to emerge from one of those plastic, chic, "hip," cookie-cutter apartment buildings that stands on the grave of a tenement building.

You want to be associated with the first wave: the artists, the junkies, the carefree, those who have as much joie de vivre as the ethnic community they pushed out. The second wave are usually students right out of college. The third wave then being younger professionals looking to live in an area with lots of singles bars, before the gay community comes in to clean the place up and make it actually nice.

We have perfected what we'd like to consider "aged housing." Just like the new t-shirt that has a vintage vibe, uses what looks like a stretched out fabric, and has a slogan about The Beatles, our housing sources wood from actual decaying slums and is covered in tasteful graffiti produced by local hooligans. Inside, however, the bones of the apartment are completely new. New plumbing, new electric, outlets on every surface, solidly constructed walls, and no sign of mold or mice. You are not too late to the party. Just because *Willamette Week* exposed this as the next best area and thus the figurative cat was out of the bag, have no fear—we have an unlimited supply of these faux finds.

Drug dealers in the entranceway are actually doormen.

Listings

Shopping

 ## SIMPLY HIDEOUS SHOES

1414 NW 23rd Avenue

New York we ain't! The rumors are true: Nobody takes more pride in less fashionable footwear than Portlandians. You won't see Manolo Blahniks, Bruno Maglis, or Jimmy Choos on these streets—clunky, utilitarian, and unflattering are the name of the game here. This must-see boutique boasts a world-class selection of Birkenstocks, Keens, Tevas, Flarts, Earwigs, orthopedic Stoons, and hard-to-find Bulgarian Glormogs. Exclusive distributor of Stuhlbargs, from Tony Award–winning actor Michael Stuhlbarg.

 ## CRAIGSLIST MEGASTORE

915 NW Kearney

Internet classifieds titan Craigslist fittingly chose Portlandia as the home of its first retail location. Featuring a wide selection of the website's most popular offerings, it's

Portlandia's HQ for slightly damaged Ikea "Billy" bookshelves, Nintendo 64 games missing their boxes, Beanie Babies, non-smoking 420-friendly roommates, and 2001 Mercury Grand Marquis transmissions.

Food & Drink

👍 NEW TUSCAN (MONDAY THROUGH THURSDAY) & TRADITIONALLY INSPIRED NEW TUSCAN (FRIDAY THROUGH SUNDAY)

251 NW 13th Avenue

James Beard Award–winning chefs Amanda and Zal Keshavarz opened New Tuscan in 2010. They split up in 2011 and so did their restaurant—arguments over the name of the restaurant caused the dispute. Upon entering you must choose sides. Do so wisely because once you pick a side, there's no going back. Amazing homemade pastas—on both sides.

NW

FUN FACT: The Portlandian alphabet has 29 letters; two of them are silent & invisible and the other is called Gregg.

HOT BERRY

924 NW Davis

What better way to warm you up on a cold, rainy Portlandia day than with a cup of boiled blueberries or blackened apples on a cone? Mashed grapes, peaches, strawberries, kiwi, banana, and grapefruit are also served inside a flaming hot watermelon. Entrepreneur Calvin Frisk refuses to close his last chain, so you better get in here while the fruit is hot! You won't find any yogurt here (or customers).

NW

Out & About

PORTLANDIA ACADEMY OF KUSO KURAE

855 NW Johnson

The first martial art developed in the Pacific Northwest, Kuso Kurae is entirely nonviolent and relies instead on the use of passive aggression. Students at the academy become proficient in cryptic text messages, glares, and intentionally audible muttering with the goal of leaving an opponent questioning his/her social status and, ideally, feeling "not so high and mighty anymore." Advanced techniques involve hostile tweets aimed at people who could never possibly see them, as well as cutting in front of someone who's driving too fast and then slowing way down.

NW

ALIKI
FARM

GOODNESS
FROM A
GOOD FARM

(OFF OF RT. 3 NEAR MCKINLEY RD)

ADULT RECESS PLAYGROUND

700 NW 11th Avenue

What comes after a lunch meeting? Recess! Let's not "kid" ourselves anymore—we all know you want to play. This 29,000-square-foot A.R.P. is located in the heart of the Pearl District and boasts adult-sized slides, adult-sized monkey bars, adult-sized seesaws, and a green space for your adult-sized bare feet to enjoy—all guaranteed to provoke adult-sized smiles! Are kids allowed? Yes, but only if they're over 21. Come be a kid again, just try not to break your arm.

NW

Portlandia by Bike

It's true what they say: You can't be a Port-landian without a bike! (See Muni. Code 382c-e 1994, fine and/or imprisonment.)

"Is Portlandia really THAT bike-friendly?" you ask. If you'd just waited a moment and

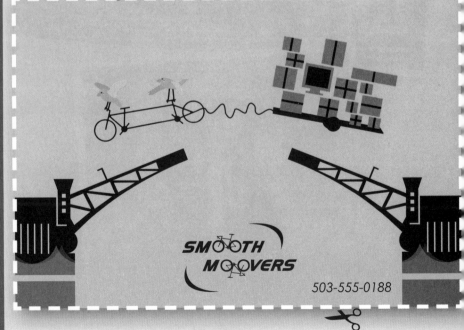

SMOOTH MOOVERS

503-555-0188

not interrupted like such a little chatterbox, we were getting to that: Yes! In national surveys, Portlandia routinely outranks cities such as Lubbock, Texas (#1,294), and Midland/Odessa, Texas (#1,293), in terms of overall bikeability, if that's even a word. In its ongoing commitment to encourage cycling, City Hall annually spends over $275 on bike paths and repainting a bike rack and bike lapel pins for custodians and cafeteria workers.

Bicycling is everything Portlandia is: healthy, green, fun, easy on your pocketbook, and loaded with opportunities for smug self-satisfaction. As a visitor, biking gives you an unparalleled, up-close-and-personal feel for the city, from its leafy greenways to its green leafyways, from its breezy accessways to its accessible breezeways, from its quiet byways to its loud bi threeways.*

So, c'mon, bring a bike! You'll feel like a true Portlandian when you pedal up a steep hill, in pouring rain, while cars desperately try to change lanes behind you.

---

*See Craigslist. Bike not required.

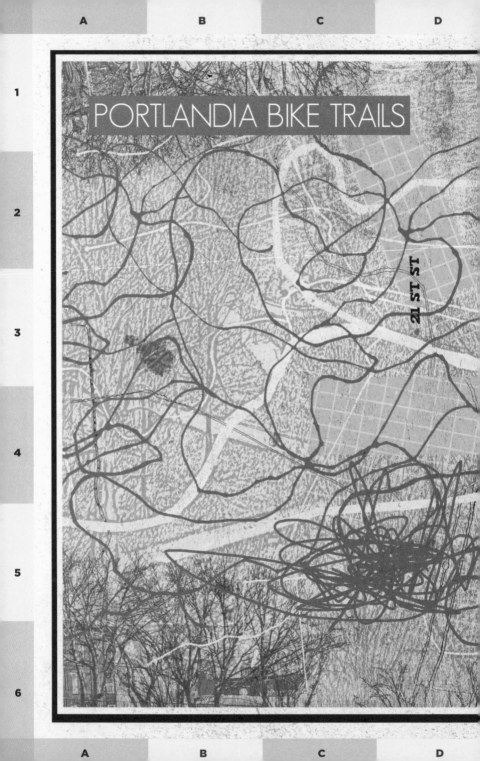

PORTLANDIA BIKE TRAILS

21 ST ST

E   F   G   H

1

2

BURNSIDE
BRIDGE

3

CITY HALL

4

WILLAMETTE RIVER

5

6

E   F   G   H

Understanding Bike Signals

Left turn

Right turn

Sieg heil

Bike like an Egyptian

Stop (in the name of love)

Look, ma, no hands

Understanding Bike Signals

Gun show

Itchy scalp

Live long
and prosper

Bike
malfunction

Jazz hands

Dos cervezas,
por favor

Check out
this booty

SOME OF THESE ARE ACTUAL LAW OTHERS ARE THE UNDERSTOOD CODE OF BICYCLE ETHICS DISOBEY AND SUFFER THE WRATH OF US, THE CYCLISTS: UNI, BI, TRI, QUAD, QUINT WHEELED

Bicycle lanes are a **SOVEREIGN** nation. Know that and enter at your own **PERIL.**

Any car lane to the left of a bike lane is also a bike lane, **IF A CYCLIST SO DECIDES.**

A motorcycle **IS A CAR.**

A bicycle slowing down indicates that **ALL TRAFFIC** must slow down.

NO honking of horns or loud music Sound pollution is **POLLUTION** (SPIP).

WHISTLE SIGNALS FROM CYCLISTS TO PEDESTRIANS:

1 ➤ Move left
2 ➤ Stay still
3 ➤ Push the person next to you over two feet to the right
4 ➤ Run forward
5 ➤ Run forward and then back QUICKLY
6 ➤ Get down and cover your ears
7 ➤ Turn around and say hi (this is a friendly gesture)
8 ➤ Turn around and then turn back around and then move left

If a car is going to make a turn, use your signal at least **FIVE** BLOCKS PRIOR.

All cars going the opposite direction of a bike: **SLOW DOWN** In fact, just **STOP.**

If your car is parked along the curb, exit and enter from your window, **NOT YOUR DOOR.**

If a cyclist pounds on your hood or roof in **ANGER** just shrug and throw your hands up apologetically.

Please note: This is a blown-up version of a laminated card that is handed out to irresponsible drivers by bicycle rights activists.

Portlandia by Car

— — — — — — — —

By car? Seriously? How could you even think of driving a car here when we have this wonderful public transit system? We even have a streetcar! And this is the #1 bike-friendly city in America, after Minneapolis? (That Minneapolis article must have been a mistake, because how can you even bike there with all that snow?)

You need to rethink this whole "car" thing. Come on.

Chapter Three

Southeast Portlandia

Introduction

By Zero Rats

Moving is something rats are accustomed to doing: Either you move or you die. But ever since we tried to hit up that Zero Packaging store we've found the perfect neighborhood—Southeast Portlandia! Something you might not know about rats—we're coffee aficionados. I mean, we don't drink it, but we do eat the beans—and the coffee bean is the most important part. Take it from a serious gorger, SE Portlandia offers up some of the best coffee spots. One of those spots is right inside our favorite bookstore—POWELL'S! They have great rat books. *Angelina Ballerina* is a classic. It's great because it teaches kids not to hate us. Oh, and their pulp book section is off the cheese! We just finished eating *Strangers on a Train*—we read it first, but then we ate it. Don't look at us like that. We're RATS! But we're cultured rats. Our favorite place to catch a good flick is Baghdad Theater. Last week we saw a movie with that white guy who plays a ukulele and sings out of tune but is handsome and has a beard and rides a Vespa…oh, and he was in some club with a mouse when he was a kid, but that's not important. What *is* important is the popcorn situation there—deeeee-licious! Hold the butter? Rat don't *think* so. Wash that corn down with a beer and call it a night. Yeah, you can drink there.

SE

Wetting our whistle is something we rats enjoy. There's one watering hole we like quite a bit. It's an actual hole, behind the thrift store. It rains a lot here, so it's mostly always full. Sometimes after a night of drinking we get a sugar jones and hit up the waffle window.

Even if it takes a while to break in, at least the smell tides us over. Uh-oh…by telling you all of this we're admitting that SE Portlandia has a bit of a rat problem. DAMMIT, we've got to move again. RATS!

SE

IF you come here,
Don't stare at us !!!
And watch where you walk,
because you are in the way
if you step into a bicycle
lane. don't be stupid!
sidewalks are technically
bicycle lanes too, look it up.
If you see a street fair,
those things are lame and
sponsored by beer companies
a much better place to
visit is Eugene, use your head,
go to Eugene!

DID YOU KNOW: Use of the Comic Sans font is a felony in Portlandia.

SE

Guide to the Best DJ Nights for the Week

Mondays: **DJ Tryst**—*great darkwave and post-punk at the Crystal Ballroom*

Tuesdays: **DJ mp3**—*great music from Dave's iPod*

Wednesdays: **DJ Pandora**—*cool mix generated automatically based on one artist*

Thursdays: **DJ GarbAHj**—*local sanitary workers spin records that others discarded*

Fridays: **DJ Direct Deposit**—*great billy, e.g. rock-a-, psycho-, Idol*

Saturdays: **DJ Mom**—*great Davy Jones solo records all night*

Sundays: **DJ LIKE IKE**—*great polka at the senior center*

DJ Don't Ask Me To Play Your Favorite Song—*plays favorite songs from '80s, '90s, and '00s—nothing you'll want to hear*

DJ Obscura—*plays "obscure" songs you've all heard but she thinks you haven't*

DJ Top 40—*the radio*

DJ Downsize—*hard rock and metal from the stock market crash year, 1987, and housing market crash year, 2007*

Wedding

So What?

SE

BAD TATTOOS
Do's And Don'ts

WE RECOMMEND YOU AVOID TATTOOS AT ALL COSTS NO MATTER HOW COOL YOU THINK THEY ARE AT THE TIME. NO MATTER WHAT, YOU WILL GROW TO HATE THEM. SINCE WE DON'T FEEL COMFORTABLE TELLING YOU WHAT TO DO.

THIS IS ONLY GOING TO BE A SECTION OF DON'TS.

IT'S TOO MUCH RESPONSIBILITY TO HAVE YOUR BAD DECISION LOOMING OVER US. IT'S HARD ENOUGH TO SLEEP AT NIGHT WITHOUT AMBIEN.

Don't...

DON'T GET A BAND TATTOO
BANDS GO OUT OF STYLE FASTER THAN HEIDI KLUM CAN SAY, "AUF WIEDERSEHEN."

DON'T TATTOO YOUR SWEETIE'S NAME ANYWHERE.
IF SHE THINKS IT IS COOL – DUMP HER– IT'S NOT.

DON'T GET AN IRONIC TATTOO
NOT EVERYONE GETS IRONY – EVEN IN PORTLANDIA.

MY FRIEND'S COUSIN LEARNED THE HARD WAY.

DON'T GET A CARTOON CHARACTER TATTOO
FIRST OF ALL IT'S COPYRIGHT INFRINGEMENT (LOOK IT UP)
AND SECONDLY, DO YOU REALLY WANT TO ADVERTISE ON YOUR BODY?
DIDN'T THINK SO.

IF YOU DO END UP WITH A BAD TATTOO THE GOOD NEWS IS YOU CAN REMOVE IT.
IT'S ONLY TEN TIMES MORE PAINFUL AND COSTLY
BUT HEY, MAYBE YOUR TATTOO COULD END UP IN A BOOK.

FUN FACT: Portlandia has two movie theaters dedicated to showing Adam Sandler films ironically.

Things to Ask Your Server When...

By Peter & Nance

Ordering Chicken

1. Is the chicken local?

   a: If the answer is no: Leave at once. Start an online petition to destroy the reputation of the restaurant unless they change their criminal policy toward the animal kingdom, which is in jeopardy because of their cruel and unusual inhumanity.

   b: If the answer is yes: Go to "2."

2. What type of diet is this local chicken on?

   a: Is the diet local *and* organic?

   b: See above, section "1," subset "a" if answer is no.

   c: If the answer is yes: Go to "3."

3. Is the chicken free range?

   a: You know what to do if they say no.

   b: If the answer is yes: Go to "4."

4. How large is the chicken's roaming area?

5. Next, find out the chicken's name so you can stop calling it "chicken."

   a: Let's call the chicken Gus.

6. How many farmers does Gus have?

7. Do these farmers pet Gus? About how many times per day is Gus comforted by human contact?

8. Does Gus have other friends besides chickens?

    a: If he's not friends with a llama, this is upsetting, but not cause enough for you to start a riot.

    b: If your server says, "What do you mean by 'friends'?", shake your head and say, "You know exactly what I'm talking about, smarty-pants."

9. If you've made it this far, it's time to get the address of the farm. Use your best judgment once you are there and try not to fall in love with the farm's leader—but good luck with that! All farms have a leader who is charismatic and has many partners. Stay on-mission,

keep it strictly business, and you should be back in your seats at the restaurant in no time.

a: Make sure they'll save your seat!

Ordering Fish

1. Is it farm raised or wild?

a: If they say farm, that's bad. Fish farms are not spacious or a fun place to fly a kite. (You should see Peter run with a kite. I can't help but want to pinch his tush.) Factory farms smoosh fish in pens and feed them pellets—this makes them fat and tasty, but it's mean to them and terrible for you. JET OUT OF THERE REAL QUICK!

b: Farmed salmon isn't even pink—THE HORROR—it's gray. That's why they shoot farmed salmon with food coloring. EEEWWWW.

c: Go wild or go home!

d: I think we're going to go home right now. The thought of Peter's tush just got us in the mood. And not the *eating* mood...right, honey? Go easy on that pedal, though. I know you have a lead foot.

Ordering Beef

1. We don't eat beef because our new pet name for each other is "little cow-cow." We can't eat each other, can we? Yes, we can. Kissy, kissy, kissy, kissy, kissy, kissy, kissy, kissy, kissy, kissy...

Peter and Nance's Guide to Buying a Motorcycle

Motorcycles + Peter and Nance = Sexy

Peter: The more wheels the better.

Nance: One wheel is the way to go.

Peter: Go on the Internet and type in "where to buy a motorcycle in (insert your town)."

Nance: Go to the shop.

Peter: Tell the shop salesman you want a bike to spice it up. He'll look at you all confused. This is normal.

Nance: Tell him you are a first-time hog buyer and he'll be really helpful and stock you up with all the goods.

Peter: When you drive out of the shop on your new chopper everyone in the store will watch and wave and laugh.

Nance: Bikers are really a friendly group, not at all like they are portrayed in the documentary *Born to Die*.

Other Must-Haves Before Your Rubber Hits the Road

Helmets? Yes.

Walkies in the helmets so you can talk to your sweetie? Yes. Kissy kiss.

Funky clothes? Yes.

Leather? A must.

New, badass attitude? Done.

SE

DURIAN

MALCOLM AND KRIS'S
CONSCIOUS
FIREPIT BUILDING GUIDE

STEP 1
GET READY FOR THE HEAT

STEP 2
BUY SUPPLIES:
STONES, GRAVEL,
MORTAR

STEP 3
BUILD YOUR FIRE PIT:
LAY OUT THE BLOCKS
MARK PIT LOCATION
AND DIG THE PIT WALLS
FILL THE PIT AND START FIRE

SE

STEP 4
RELAX AROUND YOUR
BEAUTIFUL NEW FIRE PIT

SE

MALCOLM AND KRIS'S
SUBCONSCIOUS
FIREPIT BUILDING
GUIDE

STEP 1

GET READY FOR
THE HEAT

STEP 2

BUY SUPPLIES:
CONDOMS, LEATHER
ORGY E-MAIL

STEP 3
BUILD YOUR FIRE PIT:

PAINT FACE WITH SEX
PARTNER'S DRAWN BLOOD
PICK S&M BALL GAG AND TORTURE DEVICE

STEP 4

INDULGE IN A HEDONISTIC
POLYAMOROUS PORTLANDIA
PLEASURE FEST

SE

Malcolm and Kris's Guide to Raising Confident Children

You don't need a degree in psychology to raise confident children, but we both became PhDs while Kris was pregnant. Below are some helpful tips to help your baby grow up to be a confident man- or woman-child. Good luck!

Age 0 to 10

This is the most important stage of your child's development. Anything and everything you do now will affect your child for the rest of his life—don't make any mistakes, or your child is doomed and you will be a failure as a parent.

Encourage them to do whatever they want, no matter what.

Tell them how special they are at least once an hour.

Praise, praise, and more praise. Baby poops? Say "Amazing!" Five-year-old learns to tie his shoe? Say "Genius!" Ten-year-old gets teased at school? Say "That bully is mentally challenged—it's okay; we're moving overseas."

Age 10 to 20

Oh, the terrible 10-to-20s. Your child will start his rebellion around now. That's okay. You will reign su-

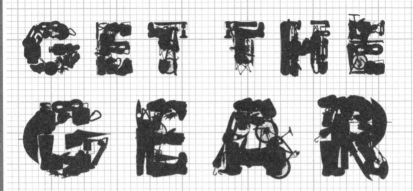

A HOW TO GUIDE BY KATH AND DAVE

REMEMBER, AN ADVENTURE IS ANYTHING THAT HAPPENS OUTDOORS.
BEFORE LEAVING YOUR HOUSE, MAKE SURE YOU HAVE THE FOLLOWING GEAR:

SE

- [ ] This checklist
- [ ] This checklist enclosed in a plastic sleeve in order to prevent water damage.
- [ ] A photocopied version of this checklist placed NOT ON YOUR PERSON,
Perhaps placed with your travel companion or in a secret compartment (think: "Kangaroo Pouch")
- [ ] A flashlight or Mag light with which to read this check list at night, or in case of a power outage or storm.
- [ ] A backpack with at least five discreet compartments--and ideally 75 compartments--in a nondescript color but with neon or boldly colored accents but that does not draw unwarranted attention.
- [ ] 4 reusable water bottles with various caps to suit one's drinking needs; one for gulping, one for sipping, one for social drinking, one for "panic swallowing"
- [ ] Chapstick with a tightly sealed cap that will not take on sand.
- [ ] Active-lifestyle, water-proof, shade-proof, weather-proof, fun-proof sunblock.
- [ ] Water-resistant coat, pants and shoes. (Rain-proof is not enough, get the ocean-proof brands)
- [ ] Land to Water back-to Land Sandals
- [ ] Toe shoes (get the 11-toed ones so that you have an extra)
- [ ] Hiking boots (Make sure they can be worn on volcanoes and not just mountains)
- [ ] A crunchy energy bar for vigorous mouth chewing and lively conversation
- [ ] A soft energy bar for relaxing
- [ ] Fire and Asteroid blanket
- [ ] Flotation Sleeping bag

preme by holding money over his head. If you don't have money, threaten physical pain—that works too, although we all know you would never do it.

Age 20 to 50

The awkward years: dating, job hunting, and retiring. If you are lucky, your child will still be living with you and you can micromanage him through this treacherous stage of development.

Age 50 to death

You are probably dead by now, so you'll need to have someone to look after your child. Or, if you see the white light, go in the opposite direction and become a ghost. Haunt him with praise until the day he dies.

SE

Gay & Lesbian Portlandia

Lesbians are kind of like coffee shops—they're everywhere! Different types live in different sections. The sporty lesbians live in NW, the hippie lesbians live in NE, the hipster lesbians live in SE, and the rich lesbians live in SW. And the gays live predominantly in San Fran and LA.

Listings

Shopping

CRUELTY-FREE PETS

2110 SE Division

As sustaining members of PETA, Fran and Noah Warren wholeheartedly believe that traditional pet "ownership" is akin to slavery. So they've carefully curated a wide selection of nontraditional pets that *need* human companionship and/or hosts to live: tapeworms, liver flukes, whipworms, eyebrow lice, *schistomiasis* bacteria and a whole "host" of other beasties. They may be hard to see and harder to love, but you'll never feel so close to your pet.

Food & Drink

SE

FREEGAN CANTINA

The Dumpster behind the Mexican joint on the corner of NW Lovejoy and NW 21st Avenue

The name says it all. The first four letters, anyway. And *free* is no longer a four-letter word. You CAN buy a free lunch here—more like take. All you need is a strong stomach, a pair of rain boots and a get-out-of-jail-free card. BYOKFP—bring your own knife, fork and plate. Fight off Homeless Al for the five o'clock all-you-can-eat tortilla chip–and-salsa special. Menu changes hourly. Freegan Cantina—diving IS allowed.

In a medium sized wooden bowl, mix flour, powder and taro root butter until it is a dry looking paste. (A cloud of powder will form over the bowl, that's to be expected). The root butter serves as a sweetener, so be careful not to add too much. Add sea salt to taste. Press segments of flour paste neatly into a cupcake pan. Pre-heat oven to 60 degrees Fahrenheit. Set the pan in for 30 minutes or so, or until you see them turn a darker beige. In a separate bowl, beat the crushed sesame seeds into a paste. This will serve as your frosting.

Add lemon juice to frosting and mix it in thoroughly. Some people like a lot of frosting, but don't listen to them. When cupcakes are ready, set them out to cool for a few minutes. Then spread frosting on top of each cupcake. The cakes themselves have a tendency to disintegrate immediately as you add the frosting, but go ahead and finish doing each one. Almost there! Then…serve! People are always asking me: "Toni what did you put in this?" Well, here's your answer everybody! Enjoy.

Poetry Critique Corner

Damian Rogers

Who are you?

THE CROSSROADS

Always put quotation marks around your title

The devil will open his mouth
and invite you in.

Carry a chicken bone, or a lion's paw.
Prepare a pot of hot soup. *And?*

Feed him and you're off the hook,
but if he's hungry, things begin

to happen. Be cool. Freeze
your face into a mask. *Use a stronger voice*

No matter where you go
there are people of power. *Where? Give an example*

There were a string of kings in Chicago
and I knew a few of them. *It feels like you are complaining*

There was a group of us
and I wasn't a part of it.

I left. I met the President
of the Middle of the Road. *Present tense? Past tense? Make up your mind.*

He wore a t-shirt advertising
rotten food and lousy coffee.

Then the bird of my mind
descended. *No*

The bird of my mind
returned to find *Love this.*

Its nest was a mess.
I ingested my ancestors.

144,000 delusional godheads
marched through my radiant inner city. *this could be: dizzy gods insane deities. Better, right?*

Now I serve the elders with both hands
and I let the fruit ferment on the branch. *I don't understand this*

switch these

— Candace

— Toni

 # Junk

1215 SE Stark

Junk provides the complete experience of a big chain store. We all grew up riding down the aisle in a cart, picking out food with mom, but today we wouldn't be caught dead in a conventional big-box store where nothing is organic. At Junk you can peruse the same merchandise without the guilt! The owners have reverse-engineered all the guilty pleasures to be healthy and made from organic and local

SE

products—like house-baked Twinkies made of classic organic-flour-based yellow cake and filled with real heavy whipping cream. They also have homemade healthy versions of popular items like Gatorade, Oreos, Diet Coke, Cheetos—you name it.

 # DIXIE VITTLES

3306 SE Belmont

Dixie Vittles presents down-home southern cooking in a comfortably theoretical setting that is careful not to recall the awkward racism and cultural missteps of the region. Mammy's Fried Chicken is presented with a short film on the civil rights movement, and the luscious banana-cream pie may only be ordered after reading a cautionary pamphlet on type 2 diabetes.

 # GRRL SCOUT COOKIES

1899 SE Morrison

After a lengthy battle with the Girl Scouts of America, riot-grrl rocker Hanna Tucker won the right to make her own artisanal Grrl Scout Cookies and reopened her brick-and-mortar outpost. Some of our faves are her tough *and* beautiful Gloria Steinem Samosas. You better not be caught alone in an alley wearing a short skirt and holding a box of Take Back the Night Tagalongs, because they are to die for. And don't forget to select some Pro-Choice Thin Mints—it's one choice you will never regret.

Out & About

👍 FUCK LAUNDRY

2905 SE Belmont

When neighborhood Chinese laundromat C. Fuk Laundry closed in 2009, Portlandia anarcho-preneur Suede T.V. Dinner saw an opportunity in the making. After switching the order of the letters on the sign, he re-opened as "Fuck Laundry"—simultaneously expressing our universal dread of washday drudgery and staking a claim as the uber-hip "anti-laundry" laundromat. The vintage facilities remain untouched, though the prices have quadrupled.

SE

👍 EAST SIDE MUFFLER

4342 SE Hawthorne Boulevard

The customer waiting room at East Side Muffler may only offer vending-machine

cuisine and stale black coffee, but overnight it has accidentally become the hip-
pest hangout in town. Pour yourself a
Styrofoam cup-o-joe alongside the greasy-
handed mechanics and lounge in a tattered
black leather La-Z-Boy while watching
Judge Judy in Spanish. If that's not your
jam, take the giant spoon bathroom key
around back and have a smoke while you
wait for the john. When you get back, enjoy a bag of Funyuns—that is, if they don't
get stuck in the machine. Shake at your
own risk.

SE

Portlandia by Car

Again? Give it up already. This really isn't a car town. Maybe you should visit LA, or like, *Raleigh-Durham* or something.

Are you aware of the damage fossil fuels do to the environment? Not to mention their social and cultural cost? Have you heard of "peak oil"? Even if you drive a Prius, you're still enabling an industry that is, let's face it, evil.

Let's just give the car thing a rest, okay?

Kids' Korner!!!

So, in an already overpopulated world, you chose to be a breeder? Um...okay, then. Presented without judgment are a few tips on visiting Portlandia with children:

Top 5 Local Schools in Portlandia

• **The Center for Early Blogging and Tweeting**

Healing Arts High

Lil' Mary Catholic Rap Academy

• Ikebana Magnet

• Ska Immersion School

After-School Activities

- **Graffiti Tagging**
- **Solstice Tai Chi**
- **Tibetan Singing Bowl Music**
- **Coffee-Cupping Workshop**
- **Willamette River Cleanup**
- **Carve Your Own Gravestone at Carver John's Crematorium**
- **Help Mommy and Daddy Petition Outside the Grocery Store**
- **Street Theater: Miming, Juggling, Squeegee-Ing, and Panhandling**

DID YOU KNOW: Portlandia holds the US record for "accidental strangulations by dreadlock."

ITEM	KEEP OR TOSS	REASON
RAZOR BLADE		
PENNIES		(SAVE FOR HOMELESS PERSON)
APPLES		
CHOCOLATE AND RAISINS	🗑	☠ (RAISINS CONTAIN SUGAR)

KEY

🎃 KEEP ♻ RECYCLE 🍦 COMPOST

🗑 TOSS DIRTY BUM ☠ POISON

Grover's Top 5

By Brendan & Michelle Marston with Grover (Yay, Grover!)

GROVER'S FAVORITE PLACE TO...

...BUY NEW CLOTHES

Grover: Where I got my light-up SpongeBob sneakers.

Michelle: But those weren't *new* sneakers, as I recall. I believe Grover dug those up from the bargain bin at this obscure little resale shop off of N. Mississippi. Remember how LA Lights were huge, in like, 1992? These are like those, but SpongeBob—early Sponge-Bob. Like season 1. Pretty rad kicks for a little kid. I didn't understand irony til I was, like, 10!

Directed by Me, Grover!

...HEAR GREAT MUSIC

Grover: *Yo Gabba Gabba!*

Brendan: Was THAT the name of that band that opened for Echo Echo? I can never remember that band name either, man! Grover and I went to this all-ages show together...some indie band that he saw for the first time at Blunderbuss, before they totally blew up on the blogs. I'm more of a punk/Krautrock guy myself, but Grover's always turning me on to new stuff. His knowledge of music is actually intimidating. You'll never forget that night, will ya, buddy? Your first concert with ol' Dad. He stayed awake for almost the whole thing.

...SPEND A RAINY DAY

Grover: Chuck E. Cheese!!!

Michelle: Did you just sneeze, Grover? God bless you! Even Grover's sneezes are a little quirky...wait, what was the question? Rainy days? Ugh, don't mention them! Grover is always dragging Brendan and me out of bed to go on rainy-day hikes! Apparently that's the best time to forage for mushrooms? I have no idea, that's just what he tells us. I will confess though, it's always worth it...he's got a great mushroom stew recipe. Grover, remind me to get that recipe from you when we get home, okay?

...GO SHOPPING

Grover: Toys R Us.

Brendan: NOT!!! Ha ha. Very funny, Grover. What a

joker...we all know where you spend your *entire al-lowance* every week. Jackpot Records is going to run out of LPs if *this* guy keeps making his bed every morning...ha ha. What, no laugh, buddy? Don't think Dad's very funny? Okay, fine, I admit I'm not as good at telling jokes as he is. He tried to sign up for improv classes, but they told him he was too young. Not cool.

...EAT SOME AWESOME FOOD

Grover: Happy Meals!

Brendan: That's what we call food from animals raised under happy circumstances. From free-range farms, and—

Grover: From McDonald's.

Michelle: We need to disconnect the television.

Chapter Four

Southwest Portlandia

Introduction

By Cat Nap

Remember how we shut down Pitchfork Media and blew the F up? Yeah, well, that didn't last. We were on stage in Berlin, our first stop on our world tour, when Gathy, our kidnapper, accidentally shot our cat and bandmate Kevin. We told her to stop bringing a loaded gun on stage, but she was all about being authentic. We understood her need to be real, but that "realness" got our Kevin killed. We had to cancel the tour and now we're back in Portlandia—which we love, but all our money is gone. Turns out Gathy *loves* the QVC shopping network. If we ever hit the road again, she's not allowed a TV in her room. She literally spent over three hundred grand on Doris Roberts's handmade stoneware. How's the resale value, you ask? Shitty. Really shitty.

Technically, we don't live in Southwest Portlandia, but we're saving up for a place here. Right now, we're living out of Gathy's van. We may be broke, but we're having a great time playing tons of gigs in Southwest Portlandia! It's coed city down here. Go Vikings! That's Portlandia State U's mascot, right? Sports are not our thing, but we've gotten lots of viking helmets thrown

at us from the crowd, so we're pretty sure the school's mascot has something to do with Nordic marauders.

Like those college kids, we're all about the cheap eats, and Southwest Portlandia has them aplenty. Sometimes we turn our van into a food cart and Gathy makes her cauliflower casserole on a hot plate. It stinks up the van but nets us some spending money. We're saving up for a hitman. The bouncer at the Slippery Pole said he knows a guy who can "get rid" of Gathy for us. Fingers crossed. Until then…enjoy SW Portlandia!

SW

Portlandia State UNIVERSITY

Available Classes

Endangered Species Topiary Design

Create beautiful horticulture art while promoting wildlife conservation. Pick from the long list of endangered species, hopefully your favorite won't become extinct before summer session.

Recycling Science

Develop a better understanding of the ever changing world of recycling bins. Includes tour of recycling center with Sanitation Twins, Marcus and Madeline Harris. **color blind students need special permission.

Advanced Pickling – "We Can Pickle That"

Learn to pickle anything from pickling experts Bryce Shivers and Lisa Eversman. Cucumbers, eggs, ice creams, dead birds, band-aids, jewel cases, tickets, broken heels and more!

Dance class: One Move

Perfect and master one of the most difficult dance moves in Portlandia. Taught by Guinness World Record holder for longest moon walk in one year.

Window Watching 101

Learn how to enjoy yourself browsing without out going inside and having to interact with annoying boutique shop owners pressuring you to buy their crappy handmade shit.

Intro to Pacifism

This class is overcrowded and since turning people away is violent and tempestuous don't expect a desk.

An Interview with the Sanitation Twins: Marcus and Madeline Harris

By Marcus Harris

Marcus: I'm Marcus Harris—

Madeline: —and I'm Madeline Harris, and we're in charge of Portlandia's recycling bins!

Marcus: And guess what?

Both: We're TWINS!

Madeline: Wow, I can't believe we got that right.

Marcus (as interviewer): So. When did you first know you were twins?

Madeline: I think it's weird you're interviewing us.

Marcus: Well, the guy from the *Willamette Week* didn't show up. He texted me his questions and said to just record it and that'd be fine.

Madeline: Why isn't he coming?

Marcus: He got stuck behind a recycling truck on SW 30th.

Madeline: Well, we've got a city to save!

Marcus (as interviewer): How did you two get into green sanitation?

SW

SW

Madeline: Are you really comfortable with me telling everyone this?

Marcus: What? Yes.

Madeline: You know that TV show, *Hoarders*?

Marcus (as interviewer): I do. Yes, I am familiar with that program.

Madeline: Marcus, my twin brother, was a hoarder. He kept bags of his fingernails under his bed, eventually those bags lifted his bed off the ground. I might get sick right now. Oh God. *Long pause while she almost pukes—she doesn't.* And I was letting it happen—I lived in the basement. Had my own entrance to the house. I ignored it for five years until human feces started leaking from above into my living room.

Marcus (as interviewer): Is that true?

Marcus (crying): Yes. I'm sorry. I was such a disgusting pig.

Madeline: Look, I know why this all happened. It's okay.

Marcus (as interviewer): What are you talking about, Madeline? What happened?

Madeline: Before we were twins...we...we...we...we...we...we...we...we...we...we (*Seriously, she really says "we" that many times, no joke.*)...we...we...we...we...we...we...were Siamese twins, attached at the back. We spent 30 years like that.

Madeline: And I realized that I wanted to have a separate life and maybe start a family, and that's when we decided to have the separation operation.

Marcus: Obviously it was successful. And even though Madeline was just one floor below me, I felt so empty and lonely and abandoned.

Madeline: That's when he spiraled.

Marcus: Long story short—Madeline had had enough and we got a truck and cleaned all our crap up!

Madeline: Your crap.

Marcus: I don't know how we lived with the smell.

Madeline: Your smell.

Marcus: Once we started cleaning, we realized there were a lot of items that could be recycled.

Madeline: And the rest is history.

FUN FACT: The City of Portlandia offers 24 different licenses for massage of inanimate objects.

FROM THE OFFICE OF:

SANITATION TWINS

WHICH BIN DOES IT GO IN?

NEWSPAPER & CARDBOARD — PLASTIC & ALUMINUM — YARD WASTE — COFFEE CUP SLEEVES — STIR STICKS

CUPS — LIDS — LIPSTICK LIDS — BROKEN UMBRELLAS — BROKEN HEARTS

LOTION — LOTION BOTTLE — FINGER NAILS — EGGSHELLS

STRIVING FOR ZERO LANDFILL CONTENT!
IT CAN HAPPEN!

Work Book: A Future Portlandia

In your opinion, which city, or part of a city, is a future Portlandia?

YOU CAN PUT A CHECK MARK NEXT TO ONLY ONE NAME.

☐ ASHEVILLE	☐ NEVADA CITY	☐ MONTREAL	☐ ATHENS
☐ MADISON	☐ LOUISVILLE	☐ OLYMPIA	☐ MISSOULA
☐ ST. PAUL	☐ SEATTLE	☐ PITTSBURGH	☐ GRAND FORKS
☐ BALTIMORE	☐ CALGARY	☐ PILSEN	☐ MESA
☐ AUSTIN	☐ SANTA FA	☐ WICKER PARK	☐ LAWRENCE
☐ ECHO PARK	☐ OMAHA	☐ THE MISSION	☐ MILWAUKEE
☐ BERKELEY	☐ LINCOLN	☐ LONG ISLAND CITY	☐ BURLINGTON
☐ WILLIAMSBURG	☐ DETROIT	☐ EUGENE	☐ PORTLAND, ME
☐ CAMBRIDGE	☐ NORTH HAMPTON	☐ SILVERLAKE	☐ FARGO

WRITE DOWN THE NAME OF THE CITY YOU PICKED HERE.

THEN COVER IT UP WITH A PIECE OF PAPER. THEN GO UP TO SOMEONE IN YOUR HOUSE OR APARTMENT, OR WHEREVER YOU ARE, AND SAY "GUESS WHICH CITY IS THE NEXT PORTLANDIA!" THEY'LL GUESS, AND AT THAT TIME, TAKE AWAY THE PIECE OF PAPER AND THEN REVEAL THE NAME WITH A HUGE SMILE. A REAL SMILE. YOU MAY THEN CONTINUE READING QUIETLY.

My 7 Favorite Places in Portlandia (Couldn't Pick Just 5!)

By The Mayor

👍 USED OFFICE CHAIR DEPOT

301 SE Water Avenue

I can spend hours sitting in different chairs, imagining myself in different jobs, leaning back (or not, depending on the chair) and reflecting on America's wasteful attitude toward old chairs.

👍 SIDEWALK OUTSIDE 919 SE ANKENY

Once found a $5 bill here!

👍 MIKE'S BIKES

1315 West Burnside

Crusty old Mike is a Portlandian fixture and a must-visit for anyone who likes to be scolded about their bike while hearing about the shortcomings of every religion besides Greek Orthodoxy.

SW

👍 MY CLOSET, LEFT-HAND SIDE

My House

Has a pleasant cedar odor and is where is found my favorite tie crumpled up (or is that crumbled up? Please check, Sam) on the floor.

24-Hour Locksmith

605 SW 12th Avenue

Comes in really handy sometimes.

Any Supermarket

Produce Section—Leeks and Kale

The sights and sounds and aromas are incredible!

SW

Junior College of Healing Arts

2555 NE Alberta

Best place in the city to get a budget-friendly massage and help a colonic student learn his or her trade while flushing undigested food particles from your intestines.

The Mayor's Fave Reggae Joint

Hello again. I'm happy you are still reading and not lost in your own little iBubble. I use the term "iBubble" to refer to all the people who have their heads down, looking at their phones and pads and whatnot, not living life. In Portlandia, we like to live and love and live again! One way I like to live it up is by hitting the fine reggae establishments Portlandia has to offer. As some of you may know, I'm the bass player for King Desmond and the Accelerators. We don't play our reggae on the reg, but when we do, we kick out the dub jams, and we do it like no one's business—the real root stuff.

My favorite reggae lunch place is the Third Beat Bar and Grill. They have excellent veggie burgers served with an enormous side of plantains. I end up taking them to go. Put them in our office kitchen and they're gone in less than five minutes. Seriously, that quick. Someone has a plantain tooth. Oh, and when they don't have a live band playing the Rasta stuff I like, they have an all-reggae jukebox. It has everything from Bob Marley to Mikey Dread. It's pretty impressive. But it could use a Zeppelin CD or two for an intermission. Just a thought.

"DUB DYNAMITE" on Thursdays at The Bungalow Club is my favorite place to cut a dub rug. I may like to play the root stuff, but every now and then I like to groove out—yah mon!—and this is the place to go. Plenty of cute girls, good-looking gentlemen, and popping music. Only issue is the lights are a little crazy for me. I'd prefer less erratic flashing. I'm not sure why they need to pulse like that—it reminds me of being in a haunted house as a kid and being chased by a man with a chainsaw. I still have the occasional night terror, where just as the bloody blade is about to split open my throat, I wake with a start, a boiling hot, sweaty mess. And forget about going to sleep after that; I'm up. Silver lining? I'm learning how to speak Italian. Bought the CDs and everything.

My final favorite is the live-music club: Caribbean Cloud. It's where my band got started and it hosts all newcomers to the scene. The open mic on Mondays is always hopping. Sign up at 7:30 p.m. and see if you can rock steady. After a hard case of the Mondays I like to come here and unwind with a $3 Red Stripe and a bowl of snack mix. Clyde, the bartender and owner, really did a good job on the mix. It's not just peanuts and pretzels. It has the dark brown bagel chips in it. I don't know what the deal is with those round guys, but they are *beyond* delicious. I'm addicted. Call *Intervention*!!! The Mayor is a bagel-chip-o-holic! Oh no, that was insensitive. I'm not, really, and I don't condone any overindulgence in any type of substance— be it food, drink, or music.

And we've come to an end. Be safe, keep cool, and don't shoot the sheriff!

Love,
The Mayor

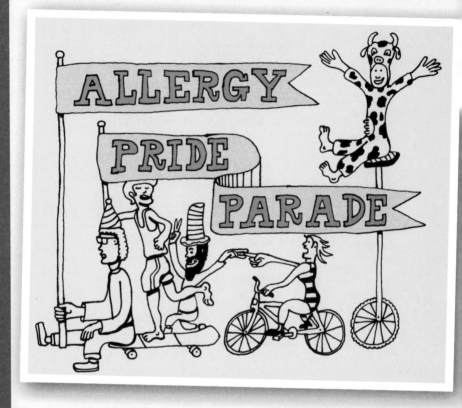

Let your freak flag fly! Portlandia's Allergy Pride Parade is a must for closeted allergy sufferers. Locally afflicted citizens, once relegated to health-food stores, acupuncture clinics and badgering waiters, now have their day in the sun (a figurative day in the sun, this year's parade was shrouded in a cloudy drizzle which turned away most spectators on account of their seasonal allergies acting up).

Rumor has it that the first APP was sparked when local Portlandian Corman Simmons stormed out into the rain after being given a quizzical look upon asking to hold the sesame seeds when ordering Sesame Chicken at a local organic Chinese-inspired eatery. Corman was not usually one to be the squeaky wheel in any given situation, but his adult-onset sesame allergy put him in the strange position of having to make special requests. The quizzical look from the waiter may or may not have been related to the request to remove the sesame seeds from the titular sesames in the Sesame Chicken, but nonetheless Corman was on the move. The makeshift parade that followed was composed of a fixed-gear bike gang, which on first sight of Corman made fun of him but upon hearing his plight took the opportunity to get anarchistic and followed him around in solidarity. One observer of the parade said it seemed like people on the street were poised to be angry about anything, and Corman's qualm became their battle cry.

The Allergy Pride Parade has not yet spread to other cities, but it seems only a matter of time. Wouldn't it be great to say you had been to Pride back in the Haight in the late '70s? Now you can. Groups usually in attendance include the Lactose Intolerant, the Wheat and Gluten Gang, the Nutty No-Nuts, the Shellfish Haters, the Cat-and-Dog Dander Dancers, the Makeup (who are allergic to makeup), the Bug Bite chapter of the Savage Riders Motorcycle Club, the Pits (who have a severe reaction to antiperspirants), and, of course, the Allergy Pride court's beauty pageant.

GUIDE TO FINDING

FREE

WIFI IN PORT LAND

WIFI IS ALL AROUND US. HERE IS A GUIDE TO FINDING IT FOR FREE ALL OVER THE GREATER PORTLANDIA AREA.

1) FOOD CART POD OFF OF DIVISION: Go behind the mini-pie food cart. There is one bar of signal coming from a resident in the adjacent apartment building. Upon writing this they still had the default "Linksys" network that could easily be joined without a password.

2) OUTSIDE THE SUEDE APARTMENTS IN THE PEARL: Right outside the "yuppie utopia" known as the Suede apartments you can get two full bars of signal coming from the concierge's setup.

WARNING:
You will only have access to the apartments intranet with the listings and sign up sheets for access to the communal roof garden plots.

3) PUBLIC LIBRARY ON KEARNEY: Anyone who checks out a book from this branch of the public library gets a free hour of WiFi access. Most people return the book immediately after their hour is up.

4) COPY PILOT: This newly opened copy shop offers free WiFi. The only downside is that there is actually no place to sit and no available outlets to plug in one's computer.

5) DIRECTLY UNDERNEATH THE ST. JOHN'S BRIDGE: if you can charter a boat for a nominal charge, then eat your heart out on free WiFi directly under the St. John's bridge. A last vestige of the Mayor's "WiFi for passing barge's" campaign, there is one last wireless router that just keeps pumping out free WiFi.

6) INSIDE THE OFFICES OF WIEDEN AND KENNEDY: Start your day by dressing as a creative professional. Dark rimmed glasses, t-shirt with a weird symbol on it and perhaps a random word kerned within an inch of its life, cool sneakers, and if you can snag one, a cool hat (check your current year for appropriate styles, upon publishing it was still the semi-ironic Sherlock) then walk the halls of Wieden and Kennedy. Just ask one of your "co-workers" for the password. Once you're online, ditch the hat so in case they are onto you, you will have less to be identified by.

SW

DID YOU KNOW: Portlandia offers more freaky, half-baked modes of public transit than any city outside of Denmark.

PA-HA! FOUND YA!:
Portlandia Adult Hide-and-Seek Association

What is Adult Hide-and-Seek? It's hide-and-seek for adults, silly! But in case you had a horrible childhood with no friends and thus were a loser (sorry Harvey Weinstein's *Bully* didn't come out 20 years ago)—here are the basics.

Object

The object of hide-and-seek is for the person who is "it" to find the players who are hiding (pretty fucking self-explanatory). In Adult Hide-and-Seek we have teams. One team hides and one team seeks (again, pretty fucking simple)—once the seeking team finds a player they bring them back to base. If they find everyone the seeking team wins, if they don't, the hiding team wins. Then, you switch. Best of three rounds wins.

Rules

- Boundaries must be set prior to starting. Example: If game is played in the PCC library, you need to specify that no one is allowed in stairwell or on the roof BEFOREHAND—got it, Garmen?
- No exploiting—where you hide must be reachable by all. Example: Garmen is "A Little Guy"—therefore he shouldn't hide in the AC vents.

PLEASE NOTE:

Our monthly "Ghosts in the Graveyard" game is cancelled until further notice. Although no one was fatally injured, the police shooting last month has put a real damper on the outdoor nighttime game.

- No moving—once you've found your spot, stick to it. If you get caught moving, you are out. That means no hiding in book bags or inside an old lady's power wheelchair basket. It may not be your fault they move around, but it's not fair. Seriously, Garmen, it's not.
- No bathrooms—it's gross. Especially when Garmen hid in the toilet tank. Not cool.

Teams

- Sherlock Holmies
- The Find Young Cannibals
- Search and Employ (Currently all team members are unemployed and looking for work—we'll do anything. No minimum wage or manual labor.)
- Punky Bruisers
- The Google Search Engineers
- Garmen's Little Guys
- The Runettes
- The Invisible Men
- The Jekyll and Hides
- Hide, How Are You?

Two Girls, Two Shirts

SW Portland - At 10th and Stark

SW

SW

GUTTERPUNKS

ANIMAL DONATION CHART

Goldfish .... → ¢ PENNIES COVER THE FISH FLAKES

PUPPY .... → $$$$

CAT .... → ££

PARROT .... → BAG OF BIRD SEED

IGUANA .... → ¥¥ 100,000 YEN NOT SURE WHAT THAT MEANS

FERRET .... → A JOINT

MEERKAT TRAFFICKING .... → ILLEGAL AS HUMAN TRAFFICKING

INJURED ANIMALS .... → BIG CHECKS

CASH

Where Does Their Money Come From?

If anyone could figure out how to grow a money tree, it would be Portlandia. But they haven't figured it out yet. So how do all these unemployed people make do? What's their income? How do small hole-in-the-wall shops in SE survive? It's a mystery. Perhaps we can find a psychic willing to channel Robert Stack's spirit to resolve this mystery. Until then, like Stonehenge, it will remain one of the great puzzles of our time.

SW

From the Oregon Historical Society Archives

January 19, 1864

My dearest Clara-Anne,

It has been two months since I have gazed into your eyes, and heretofore, one week since I have written. I hope this letter finds you cozy along the fire-hearth in the sitting room. I arrived, weary but strong, at the town of "Portlandia". The sky is grey and white, and the land defines itself with rocks and trees and many sloping green hills. The town itself is mostly Mod-ern with touches of old world charm. I was greeted by well dressed citizens who were relaxed in their manner and oddly content.

I was pointed in the direction of an Inn called "Blacksmith's" and it is from here to whichwhere I am writing this letter. It is spacious and sparse with accents of colorful art from the Kathlamet tribe. I am determined to immediately delve into the busy-ness of this great War, but am scheduled to dine with some people of whom which I have made their acquaintance for a supper of salmon and arugula salad with olive oil.

I miss you so my love.

Yours,
Joshua

January 19, 1864

Clara-Anne,

No sooner had I sent off the previous letter, and hense joined my new-friends to sup, and HAD to send this to you, to tell you that the dinner was SO GOOD. I was not told before-hand that the salmon would be covered in a roasted cashew-crust! And it wasn't arugula, it was kale with garlic bits!!! Yea! And good wine. I implore you to hear me, very, very good wine from a local vinyard. I had moe than a few glasses so, sorry for the second-letter. Anyway, I should get to bed. My room has a violin!

Yours,
Joshua

FUN FACT: 3 percent of children in Portlandia public schools receive Federal Aid because their parents speak only Klingon.

SW

February 1, 1864

My one true love Clara-Anne,

Hi! It is so great here. My days have been filled with not war issues, but breezy, relaxing days (and I believe I am getting into a bit of trouble with that. I have been receiving terse letters from various Union soldiers and ranking officials .. one was from a General! Eep!). My new friends, Britt and Patrick, do not care for the war, and roll their eyes quickly at the mere mention of the great Struggle.

There is seriously the best book-store, not twenty paces from my front door. The excellent, morning coffee has become a true habit for me, and there is an excellent piano/contra-bass duo that performs almost every night here at a pub/saloon near-by called "The Fixed Stage." Tomorrow they promised to perform only their older compositions.

I take frequent walks, and have found many places to enjoy food. They take much care in not only the preparation of dishes, but in explaining to me how they are created.

How are you, my love? Is our insane neighbor still making you listen to his idiotic stories? When I last saw him and he began to talk, I pretended that you were calling me in for dinner! Please come here! There are good buildings in the town for residence.

Your man
Joshua

SW

March 22, 1864

My beautiful Clara-Anne,

Yaaaay! That's such good news that you are coming out here! So, okay, your sister is going to send our things? I don't need that cabinet, we can get a better one here. Are you going through Chicago or St. Louis? Will you bring my grey jacket? The short one? Some tourist-travelers were here recently and they wore those ghastly wide-frock jackets with those embarassing belts, I almost said aloud "hello? It's 1864? Do you not see your reflection in a mirra?" Answer: obviously not. They probably are entertained mostly by opera house singers. Anyway...

I wrote a letter to the Union Army stating that I am no longer interested in their "war". I have a few good contacts at a design firm here to which I may be of their employ. They are working on a public space.

I can't wait to see you!

From our future Portlandia house,

Yours always,
Joshua

P.S. Britt and Patrick and I are going to start a sheet music company here. We will print only the music of local musicians! Will you join us in this endeavor?

Portlandia Police Department

2012 RTW-OTS-PUC Collection Review

(Ready to Wear—on the streets—Police Uniform Collection*)

*Only to be worn by actual Portlandia Police

By The Mayor of Portlandia

Imagine stealing a bag of potatoes from a farmer and hearing, "Stop, police!" You turn around for a split second and see two regular cops in regular old uniforms. Guess what? You'd keep running with those potatoes and you'd make it home in time for split potato stew. But if you were stealing those potatoes and heard, "Stop, police!" and turned around to see two cops in futuristic blue-and-gold uniforms that are both sleek and elegant at the same time, you'd drop those potatoes and go up to those officers and say, "My gosh, where did you get those gams!" You'd say that because the police pants are slimming and flattering to any leg. These new PPD uniforms are the real crime stoppers!

SW

DID YOU KNOW: Portlandia is the only US city to have a Comptroller with a snake tattooed on her face.

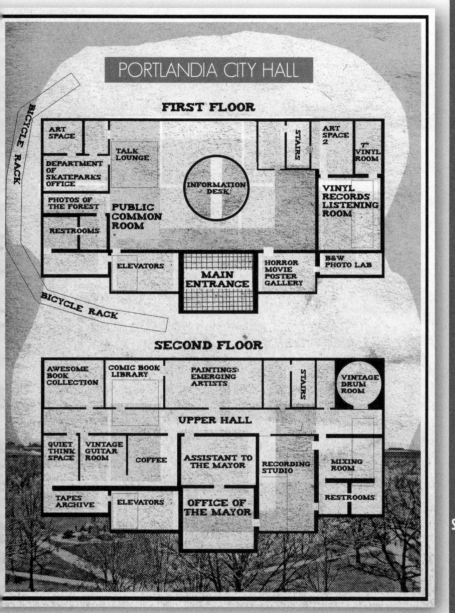

PORTLANDIA CITY HALL

FIRST FLOOR

BICYCLE RACK

ART SPACE

DEPARTMENT OF SKATEPARKS OFFICE

TALK LOUNGE

PHOTOS OF THE FOREST

PUBLIC COMMON ROOM

RESTROOMS

ELEVATORS

INFORMATION DESK

STAIRS

ART SPACE 2

7" VINYL ROOM

VINYL RECORDS LISTENING ROOM

MAIN ENTRANCE

HORROR MOVIE POSTER GALLERY

B&W PHOTO LAB

BICYCLE RACK

SECOND FLOOR

AWESOME BOOK COLLECTION

COMIC BOOK LIBRARY

PAINTINGS: EMERGING ARTISTS

STAIRS

VINTAGE DRUM ROOM

UPPER HALL

QUIET THINK SPACE

VINTAGE GUITAR ROOM

COFFEE

ASSISTANT TO THE MAYOR

RECORDING STUDIO

MIXING ROOM

TAPES ARCHIVE

ELEVATORS

OFFICE OF THE MAYOR

RESTROOMS

SW

From the simple, utilitarian desk of Chief of Police Wylie

The Mayor knows nothing about managing the police force (a.k.a is out of his mind)

Dear Governor Shelley,

Have you seen the Mayor's ideas for our new uniforms?? I don't understand him at all. Police are supposed to serve and protect, not sashay and pose. These uniforms do not instill confidence in the community that we are hired and trained to protect. I mean, where does the gun go? Or the nightstick? Or anything on the police belt for that matter! We are doing a trial run with the new (and by the way, expensive) uniforms.

I have noted immediately that: crime has risen, police recruitment has fallen and my wife has filed for divorce (that's a separate issue but still). I am enclosing some of these designs.

Pete, if we don't revert to the old uniforms soon, Portlandia might be a lawless society. You'll see people skateboarding around recklessly, playing loud music and yelling all over the place. I mean, you already see that, but you get my point.

Also, how are you? My brother ended up selling that '84 Grand National, he assumed you didn't want it after all. Thanks for asking about it!

Hope to hear from you very soon,

Chief Wylie

This is what has been presented to me!

SW

Why Food Carts Are My Life

By Randy Hobbs

When I first moved here, I didn't know anyone and I didn't cook. Now, I still don't have friends and I don't need to cook. Why? Food carts. Before food carts, I would go to eat in restaurants by myself and look like a big-ass loser. When I got tired of tables for one, I'd go to the food court at the mall. The food wasn't great, but the mall had the only comic-book store in all of Albuquerque in it. I ramble (digress).

I'm a food snob, what can I say? And food carts are perfect for foodies. You get quality food for a low price and you can sit alone and not look like a toad—it's awesome. I come every night for dinner, but I never eat the same thing. The variety is endless.

Here's a sample menu of what I might eat in a week:

Monday: BBQ cart—pulled pork sandwich and waffle fries
Tuesday: Taco cart—goat cheese quesadilla with fresh guacamole and fresh-baked chips
Wednesday: Pizza cart—fresh fig, caramelized onion and goat cheese pizza (large)—I love me some goat cheese.
Thursday: Crepe cart—salmon-and–cream cheese crepe and a Nutella one for dessert.
Friday: Hot-dog cart—the BLT dog (extra B). Side note: I'm thinking about getting an actual dog.
Saturday: Asian cart—Pho ga. It's the hangover special. I'm usually coming off of Friday night trivia at

SW

Space Lounge. I may be a loner, but I'm not a mutant. (But mutants are cool.)

Sunday: Egg cart—eggs Florentine. A boy needs his spinach—or if I'm being bad, fried chicken and waffles. Sometimes a boy needs to be naughty.

This is just a sample of what my dinner week looks like. I do lunch every day, too. For breakfast, I just eat a banana, and maybe a health bar or two. Have I gotten fat? Yes, yes I have. But, the good news is most food stations have picnic-table seating, which is good for me so I can spread out. I usually get a whole picnic bench to myself. Oh, and the cart owners are really friendly. I have a crush on the crepe girl. If I work up the nerve I'm going to ask her where she got her tattoo sleeve. I doubt I will, though. I'm a computer programmer for a reason. Guess what I want to get tattooed on my arm? A drawing of a food cart. Guess what I want to get tattooed on my other arm? "I heart food carts" in binary code. It would look like this:

```
01101001001000000011010000110
01010110000101110010011001000
01000000011001100110111101101111
01100100001000000011000110110
0001011100100111010001110011
```

Luckily, I have a whole lot of arm for it. ☺

Sincerely yours,

Randy

P.S. I wouldn't be here without food carts. Seriously, I would kill myself if they went away.

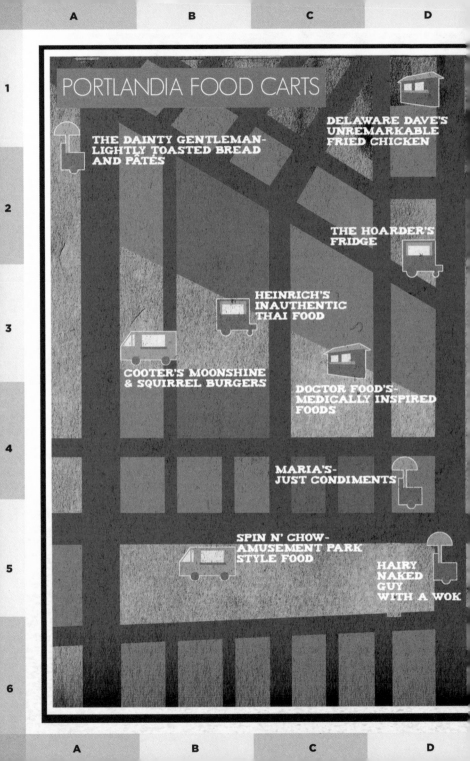

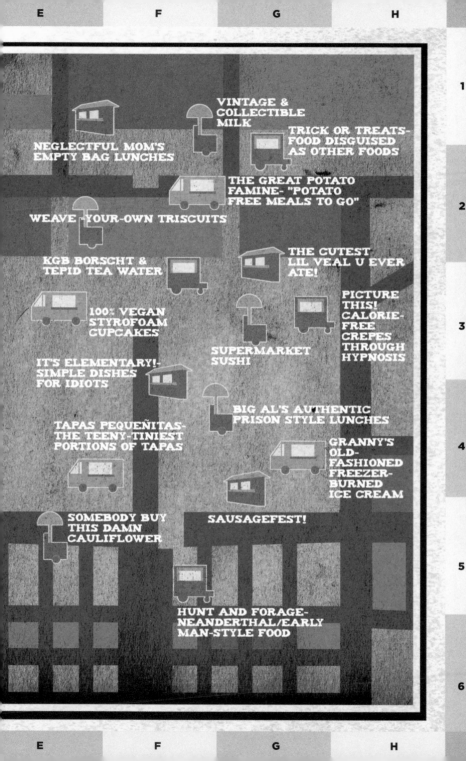

Listings

Shopping

 # Xmas 365

1011 SW Morrison

Finally Christians have something to get angry about: This store is a blatant assault on Christmas. The owners, Jezebel and Delilah, hate Christmas and Jesus so much they're trying to build a time machine to go back in time and perform an abortion on Mother Mary. Not only do they hate JC, they hate Santa, too. If you want to buy a nativity scene with decapitated camels and apostles or St. Nick being humped by Donner and Blitzen, you've come to the right place.

Food & Drink

 # Voodoo Doughnut

22 SW 3rd Avenue

The doughnut masters. They've got gay doughnuts (not to be confused with cock-and-balls doughnuts), Taco Bell doughnuts, and even cottage cheese–sprinkled ones.

SW

Fill your piehole here and you won't be sorry. If you don't try a Voodoo Doughnut while in Portlandia, we'll poke you with a stick.

Out & About

 # THE SLIPPERY POLE

322 SW 3rd Avenue

Check out this converted firehouse, where all the strippers are volunteer firefighters. Better hope they don't get called in, or you'll be running down the street with your dollar, searching for the smoke.

 # DALAI LAMA DANCERIA

230 SW Ankeny

The only dance club in the Pacific Northwest (that we know of) that promotes the teachings of the Dalai Lama and Tibetan Buddhism AND dancing your face off. Bar offerings include green tea–infused vodka and fig-juice martinis. Free Tibet and Free Jell-O shots on Saturday nights.

Lodging

 # DEUCE HOTEL

1140 SW Stark

The ultimate hipster experience...whatever *that* means. The Deuce Hotel puts the "irk" in quirky. There's so much do at this irreverent downtown staple. You can shadow one of our housekeepers for an eco-friendly cleaning ride (don't be upset if there's a line!), chill out in a deluxe room with a nap in one of our vintage grand piano beds or pull up a baby-casket bar stool and have a happy-hour drink at the authentic Speak Easy bar, but *shhhhhhh!* Get out your PETA credit card and...Just Deuce It! (not copyrighted).

SW

DEUCE HOTEL

LATE NIGHT MENU
MIDNIGHT - 6AM

KOBE MINI-SLIDERS
WITH TRUFFLE FRIES

....

MELTED GORGONZOLA SALAD
WITH CARAMELIZED ONIONS
AND MELTED BRIE

....

TWINKIES

....

CONEY ISLAND TRUFFLE FRANKS
WITH MASCARPONE MUSTARD

....

BLACKENED MAC N' CHEESE
IN A BLACK IRON POT

SW

Portlandia by Car

• •

You know what? I give up. You obviously can't live without your stupid car section, so here it is. I just hope you'll buy some carbon offsets or something. I'm going to Pok Pok (3226 SE Division).

If you're used to driving in another city, you may find Portlandia a bit frustrating at first. Motorists here don't "drive," by most definitions of the word. They coast, roll, drift, meander, and veer— but the word *driving* conveys an urgency that is considered uncouth in the laid-back environs of Portlandia.

You may be shocked the first time you encounter cars going 25 mph on a freeway with a 55 mph speed limit. But remember, that's the *limit*. Many locals prefer to reduce stress and conserve fuel by going much, much slower. Others may be on mind-altering substances, which, for their own safety and yours, require a more cautious pace. Add a blend of bicycles, streetcars, homemade vehicles, unscheduled roadwork, constant downpour, and free-range animals to the roadways and you've got a recipe for Portlandia driving!

Here are a few tips to get you on your way:

SIGNAL GUIDE

SIGNAGE	IN OTHER CITIES	IN PORTLANDIA
Stop sign	Full stop	Full stop
No Stop sign	Don't stop	Slow down to a crawl
Yield	Yield to right-of-way	Full stop
Billboard	Advertisement	Stop if interested
Bicycle Xing	Watch for cyclists	Abandon car, get on bike
School Xing	Watch for children	Children are our future
No Parking	No parking	Some parking
No Turn on Red	No turn on red permitted	Very slow turn on red permitted
One Way	One-way traffic	One-way-at-a-time traffic
No U-Turn	No U-turn	Whee!

CARS OF PORTLANDIA

VEHICLE	*Subaru station wagon*	*Toyota Prius*
OCCUPANTS	Middle-aged same-sex couple.	Advertising agency creative director or social media guru
CARGO	Dog, snowshoes, *Mother Jones*, quinoa	iPad3, iPhone 4S, MacBook Air, Stumptown Coffee, Xanax
DESTINATION	Hiking trail, dog park, yoga class, Nicole Holofcener film	Brainstorming session, pitch meeting, bankruptcy court
HAZARDS	Drivers may go 15—20 mph below the speed limit for no apparent reason	Driver may be distracted by fascinating NPR story on Moleskine notebooks

Custom vintage Volkswagen bus	Ford Super Duty pickup	Hummer H2
Snowboarders, anarcho-punks, or novelty-donut impresario	Everyone west of the Hills or east of SE 82nd	Californians
Illegal substances, dog, Flamin' Hot Cheetos	77 cubic feet of cargo space! (only cargo is yearly Xmas tree)	Flip-flops, In-N-Out burgers, attitude problems
Mt. Hood, Blunderbuss Music Festival, Arby's	Walmart, Home Depot, new Kevin James movie	Here? Oh God
Frequent stops to seek out more Flamin' Hot Cheetos	Republican bumper sticker and Toby Keith music may cause cultural dissonance in some Portlandians	Gentrification, dangerously increased materialism, shallowness, loss of unique "outsider" social status. (the #2 threat facing Portlandia, second only to Brooklynites)

Road Signs Unique to Portlandia

Simpsons Character Street Name Ahead

Falling Free-Range Chicken Zone

Lapsing Vegetarian Ahead

Spare Change?

Band Breakup

Road Signs Unique to Portlandia

Unicycle
Parking Only

Occupation Site

Park and Puff

Academy of
Clowning

Naked Bike Ride

What Goes Around
Comes Around

Local Coffee Only

Chapter Five

North Portlandia

Introduction

This chapter was omitted to save a tree.

Acknowledgments

Thank you so much to everyone who contributed to this in any way. A huge thank you to Bill Oakley and Karey Dornetto for coming up with so many new ways of looking at Portlandia. And for being so prolific. And detail oriented. And funny. Thank you everyone at Broadway Video: Jack Sullivan, Britta von Schoeler, Eleonora Monacella, Najen Naylor, Blossom Lefcourt, and Katy Jenson. Andrew Singer and Tim Sarkes for helping put it all together. Lorne Michaels for his guidance and belief in the show. Alex Baze and Tina Fey for their help.

Everyone at Grand Central Publishing for working so hard on this: Ben Greenberg, Pippa White, Dana Trombley, Beth de Guzman, and Erica Warren.

IFC for taking a chance on the show and for taking such good care of it. The cast and crew of *Portlandia*. Every department. Amazing work all around. To the visual artists of this book, thank you for creating something way beyond what we imagined: Damon

Locks, Justin Morrison, Andrew Wilcox, and Curtis Pachunka.

Thank you to the real (and dreamy) city of Portland, Oregon, for inspiring us. It's tempting to tell people to visit Portland, but at the same time we still want it to be a secret. Maybe you can visit in a secretive way?

Also, thank you punk. Punk brought us together and taught us to do things simply because we wanted to.

Carrie, Fred, and Jon

Credits

Illustrators
Damon Locks
Justin Morrison
Curtis Pachunka
Andrew Wilcox

Photographers
Dana Edelson
Danielle Mathias

Calligrapher
Margaret Neiman Harber

NOTES:

My Top 5 Favorite Bass Players

This Crazy Dream I Had

My Two Best Friends

My Top 14 Root Vegetables

A Disappointing Recipe

FUN FACT: The financial crisis
of 2008 caused a decline of over
23 percent in the city's wigwam,
teepee, yurt, and tupik values.

Things I Think People Say About Me

The Coolest Animals I Saw Today

My Drawing of a New Type of Doughnut

DID YOU KNOW: Portlandians
have voted to legalize marijuana
nine different times since 1974,
yet it remains only "mostly" legal.

2nd Chapter of My Novel

What I Remember of the Quadratic Formula

A Poem by Me!

A Haiku About Writing a Haiku

FUN FACT: Portlandia is the only city in America since the 1600s to use Public Shaming—though it is on a purely unofficial basis and applied only to clothing choices.